My Roller Coaster Life as the Husband of an Alcoholic

My Roller Coaster Life as the Husband of an Alcoholic

Neville Drinkwater

Copyright © 2017 by Neville Drinkwater

All rights reserved. This book or any portion thereof may not be reproduced or used in any manner whatsoever without the express written permission of the publisher except for the use of brief quotations in a book review or scholarly journal.

First Printing: 2017

ISBN 978-0-244-63802-3

Neville Drinkwater

neville.drinkwater66@gmail.com

To my children.

Thank you.

Without your support and patience, I would never have reached the point where I was able to tell my own story.

This is very much a true story.

I have changed all names, to protect the innocent, unfortunately this may also serve to protect the guilty, as a consequence.

Contents

Introduction 1
Chapter 1: True Romance 2
Chapter 2: Meeting the Family 14
Chapter 3: Wet Wedding 20
Chapter 4: Recycling Issues, and Children 27
Chapter 5: Moving Home 37
Chapter 6: Family Life 46
Chapter 7: On to High School 56
Chapter 8: Distances Increase 64
Chapter 9: Home Again 73
Chapter 10: A Knock on the Door 80
Chapter 11: The Merry Wanderer 87
Chapter 12: My Canal Walk 97
Chapter 13: Saved by a New Job 105
Chapter 14: The Chocolate Orange Incident 111
Chapter 15: Rehab 117
Chapter 16: Back on the Roller Coaster 129
Chapter 17: Late Night Chats with the Police 137
Chapter 18: One Day at a Time 144
My take on 'The Three 'C's' – with apologies to Al-anon 152
Alcohol – The Way Forward? 158
Epilogue 165

Acknowledgements

I would like to thank the following people, and organisations, who have all had an impact on my ability to keep going:

AA – Alcoholics Anonymous

Al-anon – for family and friends of alcoholics

Aquarius and Adsis

The BAC O'Connor Centre and Family Support Group

brighter futures

CAMHS – Child and Adolescent Mental Health Services

MIND and Younger Minds

The Pastoral Team at my childrens' High School

Royal Stoke University Hospital

The Ambulance Service

The Police officers who have visited my home

All my work colleagues, and friends, past and present

My parents, for showing me what families are all about.

Introduction

There's one in every street, could you recognize them?

I am referring to alcoholics, of course. We all have them, either in our family, extended family, or neighbourhood.

Mine was in my own home, and I was married to her. Forget all the stigma, ignominy, humiliation and disgrace, this was my wife, and the mother of my children. What the hell do I do now?

Do I divorce her and resign myself to failure, or do I fight this affliction head on. Surely where there's a will, there's a way, so I made the decision to stay by her side, or at least give things my best shot.

When my resolve alone proved to not be enough, I reasonably expected to be able to rely on some support from my wife's family. Unfortunately my expectations were unrealistic, and I was left completely to my own devices. The resulting mayhem almost killed me, my children, and my wife.

In surviving this trauma I have had to question my own sanity many times, and been pushed to the very edge of reason. I have lost count of the number of times I have been told by friends to just….let it go!

I still haven't though, and this may well be my downfall, we'll see.

My hope is that in writing my story I can open more peoples' eyes to the truth about alcoholism. Perhaps, a greater appreciation of its impact on families can start to dispel the nefarious reputation of this illness.

This is one of many ways we can hope to prevent the further spread of what I feel is a preventable plague on our society, and humanity.

Chapter 1: True Romance

'A relationship to me is never about the romance.'
Shia LaBeouf

It was a classic case of love at first sight, our eyes met across a crowded room, well a bar actually. In fact it wasn't quite first sight either. I had been admiring her from a distance for some time, so knew exactly who she was. Now we were in the same room though, and both trying not to stare, this was my chance to seize the opportunity.

It was New Year's Eve 1988 and I had been sucked in by her huge brown eyes, and......dimples. The figure hugging green dress played a less significant part, believe it or not.

The place was heaving, and there was the usual pushing and shoving you used to see back then, when pubs were still the most popular places to meet, for young and old.

After finally managing to secure my drink I carefully retreated from the bar, pint of lager in hand, high on the anticipation of the moment. As I steadily turned to face the object of my affection, who had seemingly glided over to me, I inadvertently deposited some of the ice-cold contents of my glass down the back of her dress. There was a measured shriek, maybe from both of us, then an uncomfortable silence as we slowly looked each other up and down.

Despite the embarrassment of the lager shower we did then start to talk, both of us nervously dismissing the incident. I made the assumption that she probably didn't want another drink, so didn't ask.

Later in the evening, our inevitable meeting outside ensued, and I romantically pronounced, *'I suppose I had better kiss you then'*. The world stopped turning as we kissed, and her handbag fell to the ground with a dull thud, creating just the right level of nervous awkwardness.

This was the momentous point in time which was to set in motion how the rest of my life panned out. I do wonder how different things would have been if I hadn't wowed my future wife, with my uniquely dismissive approach to romance, on that pub car park in Stoke.

What I hadn't fully appreciated at the time was that Samantha, that was her name, Sam for short, was engaged to be married to a seaman serving in the Falkland Islands.

They say love is blind, but I think it rendered me completely brainless as well. I knew she was in the process of setting up home, as my Dad was the electrician working on her property. He had been employed by Sam's fiancé through his mother, who was my Mum's ex-boss.

I found out much later that Sam's sister had more than encouraged this vision in green to make an appearance at the pub. She only lived a short distance away so had actually popped home to make a call, telling her I was there. This was before mobile phones took off, of course, and communication took more leg-work back then.

My brother also played a part as he worked part-time at the local petrol station which Sam had been calling into 'by chance', and making tentative enquiries about me. On this particular night he was working behind the bar. It seems that quite a few people were involved in the strange way fate had presented itself.

I had been consciously allowing my current relationship to die a natural death at the time. This started as a holiday romance, and we had met while swimming in the sea in Corfu.

I can only think that my holiday admirer must have been strangely attracted to my franticly bobbing head, rather than anything else. I have never been a brilliant swimmer, so can only really ever do what could be described as, barely controlled, drowning. We had been seeing each other for 12 months, but it was becoming a bind. She was a nurse in Wolverhampton so with the travelling, and her shift patterns, we were having difficulty maintaining contact.

My previous long term girlfriend before this one had run off, well more like hobbled off really, with a man who had a big nose and one leg shorter than the other. The holiday romance had been some comfort to me, as my ex and her new beau limped off into the sunset. I imagine, they went on to share a lifelong affinity with stairs, and other similar gradients, together.

I began to see more of Sam, and our covert relationship developed, my friends informed me that I was a complete idiot and my life would be ended dramatically when her fiancé returned from duty. These weren't quite the words they used, but you probably get the picture.

For this reason, when we went out on dates we would go to the more obscure, less busy places, for fear of being spotted. The fiancé had a physique resembling a gorilla and would tear me to pieces, or so my friends said.

Sam tells me she had already decided the wedding was not going ahead before we met, yet invitations, cars and venue had all been arranged and confirmed, by her parents. She had felt railroaded into the decision and had capitulated, rather than taking more time to think things through.

She told me that in her heart of hearts she had known the relationship had to end when she first introduced her fiancé to her Nana. Apparently, when they met at her grandmother's house she had said very little, aside from the fact that she didn't like the patterns on his trainers. This was enough for Sam to know that her Nana didn't approve of her choice of future husband.

I never got to see the Dear John letter written to him but I am sure it must have been a terrible shock to receive this when so far from home. This did bother me, but I was hooked, so it was not going to be enough to stop me now.

Despite my trepidation, and tangible fear of reprisals, our relationship gathered pace and we became very close. Unsurprisingly, I never took up with my friends again as they knew both parties. They felt they couldn't support me, being who they considered was the 'marriage wrecker'.

Our secluded liaisons continued and we somehow managed to avoid being spotted by any of her fiancé's friends or acquaintances. This was quite difficult as he was quite well known in the area.

We would speak for hours on the phone and do that ridiculous thing where each tells the other to put it down and then starts talking again.... *'no you put it down, no you put it down, I'm going now,...yes,... I will have to go now too...',* then we would meet up the same evening. It's a good thing we weren't still in the 70's or someone sharing the line may have angrily told us to put the damn phone down!

I had not met anyone before who I could talk to in the way I could Sam. We were both in our early twenties and found we had much in common in terms of the way we viewed the world. Many evenings were spent just sitting and talking into the early hours, with only local radio as our accompaniment. I'm sure this can't have been as bad back then, or perhaps it just didn't matter, as it was only providing a soundtrack for our canoodling.

I think I realised I had found my soul mate quite early on, as we were both loners to some extent. Neither of us had many close friends, and we didn't easily fit in with many aspects of the brash 1980's lifestyle of people around us. Our nonchalant approach to life, and the way we saw humour in things others didn't, drew us even closer, and we worked well together as a couple.

She would talk much more about her Nana, who had recently passed away, than she would her friends, or other members of her family.

Sam's school years were not enjoyable apparently. She was the rather old-fashioned girl with the big jam-jar glasses, so never really gelled with her more fashionable peers. She would spend a great deal of time with her Nana, and watch old black and white films, or read on her own. It wasn't all bad though, and Sam seems to have embraced the mainstream 80's music scene, going to quite a few big name local gigs.

She told me that, although she was happy with her job working for Post Office Counters, she had always wanted to be a Teacher. Her parents had not allowed her to re-start her 'A' Level studies, after having a bad start, so a job had been 'arranged' for her by her family.

I am conscious now that Sam's view of her childhood, and teenage years, was in stark contrast to the impression the rest of her family had of it. This was an early indicator of the underlying psychological problems she had, which were to surface later in our relationship.

As for my own childhood this was pretty normal, my younger brother has a different approach to life than I do, but there are no major problems between us. We fought when we were growing up like many siblings did, but it was all just good natured punching and kicking.

Although I enjoyed my time in Middle School, where I was Head Boy, I definitely didn't enjoy High School at all. This may have been partly due to the fact that I was one of only a very few non-Catholics, in a very highly-strung, regimented establishment.

I feel that I may have rebelled against this to some extent. This wasn't in the sense of dropping out as such, but I never really bought into many aspects of the school, and education in general, so became rather cynical in my approach to learning generally.

This meant that I probably didn't achieve what I could have done, and my exam results were not as good as was expected of me, but still easily good enough to continue with my education into Sixth Form.

I too didn't have many friends, in the true sense of the word, when at school. I tended to spend more time with what could be described as the 'odd-bods'. These were the people who didn't go along with the crowd and stood out very much for being individuals, for whatever reason.

One of these was actually very trendy and had a 'human league' style, asymmetric haircut before anyone else did, which seemed to attract a lot of interest from girls. The other was the guy with big ears who was always having the board rubber, or his homework, thrown back at him with some gusto by the teachers, in total disgust with his efforts.

I found out many years later that the slightly strange but stylish one was now in a gay relationship with a heavily tattooed man, and living on a local council estate. Board rubber man, who was widely ridiculed throughout his time in school, actually became a teacher at a highly ranked, local independent school. Who would have thought it?

Although I didn't achieve as much as I could have done academically, there were some memorable times during my High School years.

I went on two skiing holidays to Italy and Switzerland, along with our rather eccentric Physics teacher, with his archetypal tweed jacket and elbow patches. These were great, although some of us narrowly avoided serious injury or death on the Swiss trip.

Back then, I am guessing health and safety was probably not quite as important a consideration as it is now. School trips could sometimes capture the more dangerous elements of winter sports. Booking during avalanche season was certainly one such oversight.

I didn't really have much time to contemplate the merits of performing risk assessments for such holidays, as I frantically skied away from a fast approaching wave of snow, in the manner of James Bond. At least I like to think of the incident in this way anyway, it may actually have been more like Frank Spencer.

Later on in school, I achieved my Gold Duke of Edinburgh Award after four years of undertaking various community projects, expeditions, and other very worthy activities. These included a rather unpleasant four day trip into the most barren, uninhabited parts of Snowdonia.

Some of my time high up in these Welsh mountains was spent sleeping in a plastic bin liner in freezing temperatures, after losing my sleeping bag. I had watched, with a rather forlorn looking sheep by my side, as my bedding rolled and bounced in slow motion down the mountain. The sheep looked almost as upset as I was about the catastrophe, but I bet he wasn't as cold as I was during the next few nights.

It was all worth it in the end, though, as I got to meet 'Phil' himself at his big pad in London for my award ceremony, and also got to use the Queen's toilet while I was there.

After High School I tried 'A' Levels but just didn't settle down to studying well enough. For some reason I couldn't maintain the concentration levels required, so after attending two different colleges I left to join the ranks of the upwardly mobile employed instead.

I did have a thirst for knowledge and had the capabilities needed for university, but I just couldn't seem to adapt to life in further education. Anything at all would be a distraction for me, and prevent me from buckling down to the work. Even Coronation Street was enough to keep me away from my books.

The amount of studying required and, perhaps strangely, the student lifestyle, didn't really appeal to me, as I wasn't a party animal at all. My brother, on the other hand, persisted with his own further and higher education, and is now a Senior Lecturer at a University in Scotland.

When I first met Sam I was running a supermarket and doing very well for myself, having worked my way up as a management trainee very quickly. I had impressed my bosses with my commitment and energy and was given my first retail manager position at 21. The downside was I was working very long hours, including weekends.

Sam and I were both similar ages, she was just a school year younger. We had both grown up through the dire 1970's and suffered the constant strikes, power cuts and seemingly endless bad news. Then there were the anarchistic 'punk' years, and the very depressive, militant environment these encapsulated.

Whatever your political persuasion I don't think the impact of the arrival of Thatcherism can be underestimated. There was a new tangible sense of hope in the country, after years of negativity. Sharing telephone lines (yes that really happened), bumping into furniture whilst fumbling for candles, and the Austin Allegro, would hopefully now all be just memories.

If you were lucky enough to have a job in the 1980's then things had never been so good. People in work suddenly had their drive and ambition back. Of course, this did also have the downside that it encouraged the greedier elements of society to profit from this new wave of enthusiasm.

For me, though, all this meant that, being one of the lucky ones who had gained employment, I felt I now had a massive opportunity to reach my potential in life. I saw my own future as being one which would encompass all the trappings of success including fast cars, big houses and lots of holidays. The world was mine for the taking.

The beating I was expecting when Sam's fiancé returned home never happened. He probably thought it would have been too easy for him. I did once get a knowing look across the bar, and even accidentally shared a latrine with him in the pub one night. We never spoke though, and there was no real drama, as he and Sam brought their relationship to an end for good.

As we got to know each other, it became obvious to me that Sam was still definitely the marrying kind, and that I may have problems in keeping her thoughts of another wedding in check. We developed a kind of friendly 'banter' which meant marriage was often talked of in light-hearted, derogatory terms. It's still a standing joke that there was no marriage proposal as such, but instead I succumbed to being brow-beaten on the topic, whilst on the loo.

This led to some amusement years later when I met a lady who had named her property 'Trevi house', after the famous fountain in Rome where she was proposed to. I told her it probably wouldn't be appropriate to name my own house in such a way.

This aspect of our relationship was later used against me in accusations from Sam's family that I had 'caused' the ensuing deterioration in her mental health. Some commented that we had an unnatural relationship, which fostered her feelings of low self-worth.

What they perhaps didn't understand, and still don't to this day, is that gravitating towards low self-esteem was a symptom of the illness which was gradually taking over Sam's mind, and had been for years before we met.

Placing herself in low moods and blaming others for the situation she then found herself in was, unbeknown to me at the time, evidence of a very serious long term health issue. It would not have mattered one bit how I conducted myself with her, as this condition was already entrenched.

As the two of us got to know each other better we found we had many shared interests. We both loved the theatre, and particularly musicals, we had a keen interest in current affairs and politics, and also enjoyed watching live bands and eating out. With two good incomes we were able to indulge ourselves and had a great time together, in a very conventional way. As the disposable income was available I wanted to enjoy this privilege, and have something to show for my hard work.

I had always hankered after a sports car and had been reading for some time about the Mazda MX5, which was due to be launched in the UK. It was right up my street, being a classically styled, two-seater convertible, with pop-up headlights. This was way before it developed somewhat of a reputation as a 'hairdressers' car in later incarnations.

Cars with character had always appealed to me and I had previously owned a Mini and a VW Beetle. I also had a Dutton Phaeton kit car when I first met Sam. This was an absolute death-trap, much like a bath tub with an engine attached, but great fun. This car had to go unfortunately, as driving it in the rain resulted in a dirty shower, with road spray jetting up your trouser legs, or skirt, as the case may be.

For some reason Sam never really warmed to outings in the Dutton, and the need to pick the dead flies from her forehead after returning from a high-speed blast in it.

The Mazda salesman was quite taken aback when I walked into the showroom and asked him to order me an MX5, in red. I had found out all I wanted about the car beforehand from the motoring press.

He was trying to launch into his sales pitch which he must have been practising for some time, but there was no need, I knew I wanted the car before even seeing it properly. There was a six month waiting list but I was still one of the first people in the area to have one.

We had some good times in the MX5 and I loved the whole 'wind in the hair' experience. There were a number of road trips, one I recall to the Yorkshire Dales, which was fabulous. We toured the Dales and stayed in a stunning Art Deco hotel in York. Both of us had an appreciation of architecture and design, so would take pleasure in looking around period buildings and stately homes.

I had a very expensive in-car hi-fi fitted, with amplifiers under the seats and a huge sub-woofer speaker box right behind our heads. What rebels we were, tearing up the countryside with our deafening, middle of the road music, upsetting all the cows.

As I was concerned about parking my car where I worked, Sam would take the Mazda, and I would use our old Mini in the day. This meant she could go posing on her own, to and from work. She was always a good driver so I didn't worry too much about my pride and joy.

This probably gave credence to many peoples' view of our relationship, in that they perceived Sam 'wore the trousers'. This thinking may also have been reinforced by the number of times I would be down on my knees in front of her, even in public. I wasn't bowing to her commands, just constantly having to look for her contact lenses.

Sam did have a very, very stubborn streak though, which meant she would rarely back down in an argument. This was to cause her problems later in life, when she would not listen to, or act on, the advice of medical professionals.

The inevitable pressures of our burgeoning relationship took their toll and we had an off-spell. We did have some pretty volatile quarrels, and like many couples this eventually reached a point where we both needed a break, so we parted for a while.

The separation didn't last, largely because Sam turned up at my Mum and Dads house on a regular basis over the next few months, with any excuse to see me. She wasn't going to let me escape her clutches.

After a few of these meetings Sam arrived one evening to supposedly return a set of stepladders she had borrowed. It transpired that whilst she had remembered the stepladders, she seemed to have forgotten to check how much underwear she was wearing.

We were back together again.

Chapter 2: Meeting the Family

'Families are about love overcoming emotional torture.'
Matt Groening

I was introduced to Sam's family very soon after we started seeing each other, and found the whole thing quite daunting.

They all seemed to be wrapped up in themselves, and only talked when they had a glass in their hand. The gatherings were very loud and quite intimidating. They were also not what could be described as inclusive or particularly polite, in fact I spent the next 27 years still feeling like an outsider.

Conversations all seemed to revolve around what happened the last time they got together drinking, how much of it was consumed, and what kind of state they were in before during and after. Oh, and football, which I could not describe myself as a huge fan of, although I did follow the local teams, in a very uneducated way.

I was not used to this at all, as my own family would not usually drink or talk in quite this way. They did drink, but alcohol was certainly not a statutory requirement for any get-together with them. When I was growing up in the seventies drinking was something which only really happened in pubs or, at special events. Drink for consumption at home would only be bought very occasionally from the local off-licence, in the evening. Even then, this was only ever as and when required, rather than being stocked up in the house.

There was definitely no large supply of alcohol in my parents' house and still isn't to this day. I therefore found this whole attitude to alcohol both unusual, and a tad inconsiderate of those who didn't feel the same way.

Like anyone of my age I enjoyed a drink, but only really when out socialising, or at a party of some kind, not as a matter of course when at home with family.

Sam was the youngest of three sisters but was the only one to have been given just one first name. She told me later that she was supposed to have been a boy, named Dominic, to continue the family line. Her father was the last male with his surname.

Her middle sister, Wanda, apparently used to tell Sam, as a child, that she had been adopted. Was this sisterly banter, or something much more damaging? Who knows? What I do know though, is that various psychologists and therapists would later have a field day with all this.

One of Sam's friends from her time with Royal Mail, to this day, still fills in the name gap for her by calling her Samantha Jane. They have known each other for over 30 years now, and he has always empathised with her sensitivity on this topic.

Being rather naive as a teenager, Sam told me she had been mocked and ridiculed by her older sister, Sandra, and her future husband, Sean. It seems that, as a group, boyfriends included, her sisters had derived some pleasure from rather infantile pranks at her expense.

Sam had always walked and talked in her sleep, and on one particular occasion they tape-recorded her dream-talking. Then they replayed these recordings at separate times to other members of her family, purely for their own amusement. Perhaps this was funny at the time, but it was quite obviously very much the wrong time for Sam. This was during a very impressionable period in her tricky adolescent years.

These childhood memories, along with others I have been told about over the years, were indicative of Sam's lifelong struggles with self-esteem, and she often replays them to this day. They have left an indelible mark on her character, and particularly her long term mental health.

The only positive memories Sam talked about were those involving her Nana. The stories she told of the things they did together, were what would more usually have been expected of a mother and daughter relationship. They had obviously been very close.

Oddly though, she has also divulged that it was her Nana who gave her a taste for alcohol in the first place. She would often be given a 'tot' of whatever spirit was available as a child, as I suppose may have been common practice in some families.

Early in our relationship I was invited to a family meal for Sandra's birthday, at a local Greek restaurant. I was driving, so landed the job of giving her and Sean a lift home.

The drink flowed, and towards the end of the evening it transpired that Sandra was in the restaurant toilet in a state of inebriation. She had to be literally dragged out of the toilet by her sisters to get her to my car. This was before I had the Mazda. Anyway, as she was bundled into the car she proceeded to immediately throw up on it.

This was the very first time I had been out with my future wife's family, and was also when I realised that they all had such a strong relationship with alcohol. It wasn't really what I would have expected for an evening out where the new boyfriend had been invited, but this obviously didn't figure in their thinking.

After attending subsequent family gatherings, which were largely held at Wanda's house, I realised that these all tended to be stage managed. There were rarely any of the small relaxed chats that most families have, there always had to be the big event, with a houseful of people, some of them not even family.

There was a palpable tension between Sam and her parents at these house parties, which I put down to the stressful surroundings, but which would actually prove in time to be a much deeper issue.

When we had visits at our house later in our relationship, which were almost exclusively on birthdays, I would feel obliged to buy in red wine. Even on the rare occasions when we had visitors outside of birthdays, I still felt I had to have wine available. Alcohol always felt like a pre-requisite to any of Sam's family removing their coats.

It soon became apparent that Wanda was the one who liked to be in control of all the family events. She revelled in the whole entertaining and attention thing so rarely did anyone else try to take the lead. There was usually something new to show off about on everyone's arrival chez Wanda, which would often be the main talking point for the evening. Wanda was a retailers' dream and was always buying something, or having something new done to the house. This sometimes felt much like product placement, and I half expected a cheesy salesman to pop out of the gathered crowd, pen in hand.

Sandra was much less materialistic, more reserved, and not so overbearing. Both sisters had three children, Wanda had a boy and two girls, and Sandra had twin boys and a girl.

Although the age gap between the three sisters was not huge, at times it did almost feel like we were a generation apart. In the light of the ages of their children I suppose they were a decade or more ahead of us in life, which did make a difference.

This was another barrier to conversation, along with the divergent interests we had. Try as I might I could not hope to engage in any kind of detailed discussion around the finer points of the offside rule, or how many drinks it took to put me on my back, for that matter.

Don't get me wrong here, we never fell out or argued at all, I just often felt rather disengaged, and very much outside of the clique. My own sport of choice was Formula 1, and there was nobody else in the family even mildly interested in this. It wasn't their fault, but they certainly never made the same efforts to accommodate my interests, as I did in attempting to understand the merits of a flat back four.

I had managed to get Sam interested in motor racing though, but I think this was mainly to do with the celebrity aspect of the sport, more than the actual racing.

We did go to one classic Grand Prix together in 1993 at Donnington, where we had the pleasure of witnessing Ayrton Senna at his very best, only a year before his untimely death. He won by a whole lap over Damon Hill, in the rain, whilst Michael Schumacher, still in his learning curve at that time, span off the track into the gravel trap, right in front of us. I have always wanted to go to Monaco to see the Grand Prix there, maybe one day I will.

Sam's parents were both retired by the time our relationship got going. They were only in their mid-fifties so hadn't had a hard life as far as I could tell. My parents both worked into their seventies, and my Dad still does some work even now. This is probably to do with the fact they had ploughed all their available money into extending and improving their own property over the years, whereas Sam's parents hadn't.

Sam's mother was partially deaf, although often this seemed to be selective deafness, and she could certainly lip-read very well. It did mean that she was very loud though, although so was Sam, and Wanda at times, so this may have simply been genetic.

Sam's parents were revered by Wanda and Sandra in a way that I haven't seen before or since, which included them being protected ferociously from any form of bad news.

I picked up on the *'don't tell Mum'* philosophy of her sisters early on. They only ever wanted their parents to deal with the good stuff, like Christmas, where they were alternative Santa's for their grandchildren.

There was no doubt they were very good providers, and everyone was very well catered for materially. The children and grandchildren never went short in terms of presents. It did almost become a competition for how many gifts could be bought in one go, for one person.

The way Sam's parents would completely avoid involvement with anything at all contentious though, was to become more and more of a problem to me as I became part of the wider family. I soon learnt that they could not be turned to at all in a crisis. It just wasn't what they were about, and even if it had been, they wouldn't have been allowed to step up to the mark without Wanda and Sandra taking over.

Chapter 3: Wet Wedding

'Marriage is a wonderful institution, but who wants to live in an institution.'
Groucho Marx

We went on to have almost five years together as a couple before we got married. Sam wore me down gradually and bought her own house to instil my own sense of nest-making. It worked, and despite more than a hint of rebellion from me, we married in Cyprus in 1994. It was my decision to marry abroad without any family present. I think I was still fighting with my own feelings around the finality of a long term commitment.

This didn't go down well with either set of parents, but we did it anyway. We did, though, have to arrange a church blessing and reception in the UK on our return, to keep everyone happy. In hindsight, I think I may have preferred a traditional wedding in the UK after all.

It rained heavily all day long for our wedding in Paphos, the only time it did so in the whole fortnight we were there. The locals were keen to tell us this was a good omen. I wasn't totally convinced though, I think they were just trying to humour us.

A rather large, unshaven, Cypriot man followed us around all day with a video camera, which was very disconcerting. As there were just the two of us for most of the time it became more than a little weird after a while. He attempted to make us the centre of attention at every opportunity. It made it all a rather unsettling experience, with lots of people we didn't know watching us intently.

The video of our wedding ceremony at Paphos Town Hall makes us both howl with laughter when we dust it off occasionally. A couple from Birmingham we met there were our witnesses, and the expression on their faces was almost as funny as the one on mine, I looked like I had just had a stroke.

Prior to our wedding we took a mini cruise from Cyprus, for a whistle-stop tour of Egypt and The Holy Land. I had always been interested in ancient civilisations so was looking forward to seeing the Pyramids, more than anything else on the trip.

When we arrived at Giza we were ushered towards the awe inspiring structures, and then into a queue of excited people waiting to enter the Great Pyramid. As we got closer to the entrance a sudden fear of foreboding swept over me, and I had what could only be described as a panic attack. This seemed to have been brought about by the mere thought of what was to come when we were inside the tunnels and chambers. I found I was unable to entertain the thought of going any further and had to escape.

I had never suffered anything like this before but had become frightened of the very claustrophobic conditions being presented to me. There was a very narrow, pungent, corridor which we were being forced into, carried along by the raucous bustling crowd. The smell of a thousand sweaty bodies was just too much for me, and I had to walk away from the queue just as we were about to enter.

When I think back to my irrational reaction to the Great Pyramid I cannot help thinking this may have been a metaphor for my fears around my impending marriage, and my life to come.

We returned home as man and wife, but had to go through the 'second wedding' for our families. I must admit though, that I found this more enjoyable than the one in Cyprus. My very paranoid approach to being on show had been uncalled for after all, and I did have a good time.

I had already moved in, and made our small terraced house home a few years before, so there was no big change to become accustomed to after we were married.

We did have quite a tempestuous relationship, which was often punctuated with aggressive outbursts from Sam. She would quite often fly off the handle over the most insignificant aspects of ordinary life. I suppose I must have learned to live with this to some extent, as she was absolutely fine between these attacks. I put it down to her hormones some of the time.

One particularly memorable episode, before I moved in, had resulted in a hammer being thrown across the street at my car, whilst I was driving away to escape her anger. Luckily it missed, and flew past onto the other side of the street, just inches from the roof of my beloved Mazda, and my head.

On another occasion she virtually threw my brother and his then girlfriend out of the house, in an unprovoked attack. Sam always did aggression very well, and still to this day has the kind of piercing shout that could shake foundations.

I never really associated any of this with drinking, but now that I reflect on these times, the signs were all there even back then. The unfortunate thing about addiction is that it can creep up on someone over a very long period of time and gradually, by stealth, the illness takes control of their faculties, judgement, and even their personality to some extent.

As the husband of an alcoholic you tend to not want to accept there is a problem at all, particularly as there is no solution for it. Everyone drank back then, as they do now, and it was also becoming ever more popular to drink wine at home, so it was completely acceptable.

What I was not understanding was that my wife's brain was being adversely affected by alcohol, and some of the damage would be completely irreversible.

Some people can drink their whole lives and never have a problem with their health, or so they will always say. In Sam's case she was susceptible to addiction due to her underlying mental characteristics, which had been shaped in her formative years.

I liken this to playing Russian roulette, in that when we drink we all hold guns against our heads, but only some of these will ever be loaded. My wife's gun was loaded unfortunately, and she fell into addiction. I actually think that Sam may have taken a bullet for the rest of her extended family, it was bound to happen to at least one of them by the law of averages, as far as I can see.

The accepted definition of alcoholism, by Alcoholics Anonymous is:

'A physical compulsion, coupled with a mental obsession'.

Anyone with the required level of vulnerability, who drinks either regularly or heavily, can cross the invisible line into compulsive behaviour at any time in their lives. Then there is likely to be no way back.

Once the habit is embedded into behaviours it is only one small step to dependency, and then full-blown addiction. If you cannot cease drinking for any significant period of time then you could already be alcohol dependant, and so potentially living on borrowed time.

Alcoholism is like a box of chocolates, to paraphrase Forrest Gump. If you are lucky you will end up as one of those who is, 'no trouble to anyone' and just sits and slowly drinks themselves to death, without really bothering other people. I have a friend whose son would, unfortunately, fall into this category.

Alternatively, you may become one of those happy, friendly drunks who many of us know. This type tends to die unexpectedly and then it all comes out into the open about their habit, and what their real story was, after their death.

Then there is the type my wife was eventually to become after many years, very much in the vein of Jekyll and Hyde. The end result for these is very often the same as the other types. The difference is they are more likely to take their families along with them, for one hell of a bumpy ride.

Sam had actually fallen into compulsive and obsessive drinking from her late teenage years. Even her 'non-secret' consumption would often involve drinking heavily on nights out. This would include stockpiling drinks in pubs at closing time, and even driving to other parts of the city at full pelt to beat even a slight difference in licenced hours. All unbeknown to, or ignored, by her parents.

When at home, she would take wine from their 'Country Manor' wine boxes which were kept in the fridge at that time. There was a free and easy approach to alcohol at home anyway, so they would not have thought it unusual for her to have a glass in her hand. She would then take this up to her bedroom to drink on her own, returning for regular top-ups.

Although alcohol was not sold as widely as it is now, it was easier to get served in both shops and pubs, at that time, than it is now. This was particularly true of females, who were rarely challenged to prove their age. Once she was working Sam could easily afford to replace the wine boxes in the fridge with new ones, so that her parents didn't realise just how much she was drinking.

This kind of behaviour was the start of Sam's path into addiction. The secrecy and scheming, which would become much more prevalent later in life, as her illness took hold, was already well established as a teenager.

It had nothing to do with *how much* she was drinking, or *what* it was she was drinking, but rather *'why'* she was drinking. Anyone who begins to drink alone in their room during their formative years potentially has a big problem. The *'why'* part of this is, of course, very contentious. There were, as I understand, a number of key events in Sam's life at around this time which unsettled her greatly. Was this to blame, who knows, but there is one thing I am certain of:

Her family choosing not to talk about all this with her properly, for the next 30 years plus, didn't help matters at all.

This is not the only thing which has never been openly discussed in Sam's family. Whenever any, even mildly contentious, topic was raised, her protestations would be literally shouted down by her sisters and mother, in unison. Any negative perceptions or feelings would be dismissed immediately, especially if these referred to her childhood.

I found this both odd and very contradictory, particularly as for as long as I have known her, Sam has been called on in the role of family oracle. She was the one they would all turn to if they wanted to recall people and events from the past, as it was always widely accepted that she had by far the most accurate recollections.

It must have been disturbing for Sam then, to find that her parents and sisters would question anything she remembered which involved her own personal feelings. It seems only their own sentiments about the past were relevant at all, and not hers.

There is an event from around this time which will always stick in my mind. I suppose the reason is that it illustrates the very different way family issues were dealt with by me and Sam, when compared to the approach of the rest of her family.

One Saturday morning, when we were at home, Sam came to me in a state of abject panic. She said that there had just been an announcement on the radio and we needed to go and look for Wanda's son, Brandon, who was missing from home, and in some sort of trouble. We got straight into the car and headed for the town nearby, where he was 'on the run', with the intention of us reasoning with him to go home.

After parking in the town centre I caught sight of him and gave chase. Unfortunately I lost my footing whilst running at full speed up the hill out of town and, embarrassingly, fell heavily onto my hip. I still have the scar from this waterless belly-flop to this day.

After picking myself up in front of a crowd of people, who must have been quite entertained by my acrobatics, I continued the chase, but had lost him. We both tried to carry on the search but without success, so returned home. Sam later had to enquire with Wanda as to whether he had been found, which he had thankfully. However, to this day I have no idea what this was all about, as it has never been mentioned since by any members of my wife's family.

I think this may be one of the main differences between myself and Sam's family. I have always worn my heart on my sleeve and no subject is taboo for me, whereas I feel they have all, conversely, lived a life positively brimming with secrets and lies.

They prefer to keep their feelings in check and will never entertain talking about them, no matter how important these may be to the person or persons involved.

I feel this has allowed some members of Sam's family to live a life based entirely around materialism, seemingly lacking any soul or emotion, and with the depth of a puddle.

Chapter 4: Recycling Issues, and Children

'You can't have everything……..where would you put it?'
<u>Steven Wright</u>

These were the days when empty bottles had to be taken to the bottle bank, as there was no street collection for recycling. Visitors and neighbours would comment on the number of empty wine bottles I was having to load into the car on a regular basis, and which were stacked up in our kitchen. Although I recognised the amounts I just didn't appreciate the underlying problem at all.

We usually ate together quite late due to my work, and both drank a glass or two of wine with our meal. However, what I hadn't understood was that Sam had often been drinking before I got home and would continue for some time after I stopped. She was probably consuming more than a whole bottle to herself each night.

This in itself though, only raised the issue of affordability with me, rather than the more serious problem of addiction, which I had simply not considered. We would often talk about cutting back on the wine as it was having a serious effect on our finances, but never really discussed the impact on our health. I was not a big drinker but must have at times assumed I was, due to the sheer volume of empties I was having to dispose of.

We had a joint bank account from quite early in our relationship, so it was difficult to separate our expenditure, particularly when we were renovating the house, and had various projects on the go.

It is only relatively recently that I have begun to understand why we have never been well off, despite having two incomes for the largest proportion of our time together.

I have estimated that Sam's drinking, and all the associated costs has lost my family well in excess of £300,000 just over the last 20 years. This could have been used towards a better house, or the simply the various trappings of financial security which most people of our age seem to have.

Our home has not been decorated properly for over 10 years, we still have an old tube television and have had very few holidays. We have mortgage and personal debts amounting to above £165,000 in total, and a house worth about the same. Most people I know my age are far more sorted than this financially. Having an addict in the family is a very expensive business.

By the time our first child was on the way in 1995 it was starting to dawn on me that Sam had a real problem with alcohol, although I still failed to recognise the much deeper problem of addiction. She had great difficulty ceasing drinking during pregnancy and would attempt to justify reducing her intake, rather than completely stopping, as advised by her GP and other health professionals.

There were no real problems with the pregnancy though, and Jack Alexander was born in June 1996. We gave him his middle name in homage to the 'Alexander the Great' hotel we stayed at in Cyprus.

I was there at the birth, as I was with all our children, and everything went well. I could never have envisaged myself in this position at all. The position being…..watching what was to become my son emerging amongst a grotesque mess of blood and ooze….., from between my wife's legs. I don't think anything can really prepare you for that rather gory display.

I had never really bought into the thought of having children and had been in a form of denial up to this point. When it happened though, I soon came to realise that this was definitely it, and there was no turning back now.

I surprised myself by taking to being a father like a duck to water, and soon found I had to be hands-on. Sam would often fall asleep whilst breast-feeding and I would need to rescue Jack. Occasionally he would roll off the bed having dozed-off with his Mum, but I don't believe he was ever harmed. It may have accounted for the fact that he did go through a phase of having a rather square head for a while, though, who knows?

The drinking didn't ever stop completely and I did become worried about the effect of this on Sam's breast milk. For this reason, and a degree of convenience, we began to use formula milk as well. I would take over feeding duties when Sam wasn't fit, or sometimes just because I could.

In the many hours Jack spent resting across me while I fed him, I felt him become part of me. There is a bond which I think can only be experienced by a father and his first born, which then defines who you both are from that point onwards. This boy was going to go places, be somebody, and we were now a proper family, and not just two people muddling along through life.

It may have been using formula milk which helped, I will never know, but there does not seem to have been any long-term damage to any of our children from alcohol. I have heard some terrible stories over the years about the harm it can cause but there have been no noticeable, or diagnosed, ill effects luckily.

Jack was a happy baby and we seemed to cope well as a new family, with Sam returning to work after maternity leave, and her mother helping with pre-nursery childcare in the daytime. She was a retired Nursery Nurse so we felt this was a better option than going private.

We did look at some private nurseries but these did not inspire confidence in us at all. Both my parents were still working so we couldn't ask them for help with childcare in the daytime. We paid

Sam's Mum for her help, but she would set this money aside towards our holidays.

This all sounds great and to a large extent everything was fine. However, from the very first time I met Sam's parents I knew there were longstanding tensions between them and their daughter.

Once we had a baby, there just wasn't the closeness that you would expect from a parent when you had given them a grandchild. Perhaps it was because this was now all 'old hat', being the seventh one for them. Sam had quite obviously presented her parents with a problem which they had great difficulty with. She had not followed the pattern of her two older sisters in settling down at a young age.

This had impacted on their very long term retirement plans, unlike her sisters who had married quickly and provided grandchildren for them early on, so conforming to their expectations. In fact, being a non-conformist had been somewhat of a theme in Sam's life, and it seems her parents were unable to cope with any disruption this caused to their own master-plan.

At the age of 19 Sam had to have an abortion as a result of a failed relationship. She was marched to the abortion clinic by Wanda, who seems to have been given all the parental responsibility, from Sam's mid-teens onwards.

It does very much seem to me that as soon as Sam's mother and father first became grandparents, they chose to cease being parents completely from that point on.

Their delegation of responsibility has continued during the whole time I have known them, and they have never shown any accountability for anything that has happened in Sam's life.

I have constantly been told that she was spoilt as a child. I have no doubt whatsoever that she was spoilt materially, but I believe she may have been starved of any degree of parental affection, which set out the stall for her future problems.

Despite all this history everything proceeded largely without incident whenever we did meet up with Sam's family. We all got on well enough, on the surface at least, and there were usually too many people in the room to ever have serious arguments.

The other thing to bear in mind is that, in a situation where family meetings were centred wholly on either the children, or the big event, there would be very little scope to enter into any meaningful adult discussions.

Visits to our house, by Wanda together with her husband Terry particularly, dried up after a short time. We have photographs of them in our house, up to when the children were toddlers, but none beyond the early 2000's. They just stopped visiting as a couple and only Wanda would call briefly, almost exclusively on birthdays, usually on her way home from work.

This became an issue for Sam in particular as she felt that we weren't good enough, and neither was our house good enough, for her middle sister and her husband. It is very important to appreciate the significance of this, as it has been a key factor in Sam's overall mental health.

As a sufferer of low self-esteem her whole life she was always seeking affirmation of her abilities as a homemaker, amongst other things. When visits from her sisters and their husbands mostly consisted of them only 'popping in' at best, this had a detrimental effect on her state of mind.

There was also an issue with the body language from Sam's parents and sisters. This can be a very powerful weapon, and should not be under-estimated in terms of its ability to influence outcomes of all sorts.

The way we project ourselves in front of people will often say much more than words, and is particularly true when you are a guest in someone's home. Not sitting down, or perching on the edge of a chair or sofa, sends a message that you don't really want to be there. Refusing a hot or cold drink of any kind also sends a similar message. As for not removing your coat, well this is just about the most blatant signal you could give to anyone, that you have no intention of giving them much of your time.

In many of the very rare visits we had from Sam's sisters this was how they conducted themselves. Their approach always gave the impression that they would not be staying very long, which I know caused her some distress. Even years later, when the whole family was aware of Sam's poor mental health, there was no attempt made to adjust their own behaviour accordingly.

As with any illness, you have to accommodate the person's needs where you can, and it wasn't ever hard to grasp that she was unwell. Her mother and father surely must have known, but they demonstrated the very worst kind of body language. They didn't even leave their own house, so couldn't have sent a stronger message.

For many of us it is essential from time to time that we are able to relax and feel completely comfortable, in whatever setting we are in. Understandably, most would say that the best chance of this happening is in their own home. If a grown-up discussion is needed then someone's own home should be the first option, as this is their comfort zone. They are unlikely to open up so readily when outside of this, and cannot be expected to act like a performing seal when required to.

Sam suffered from agoraphobic tendencies which meant she would become nervous even when leaving her own house for the uncertainty of someone else's. Especially if there were going to be people there she didn't know very well. The nature of her illness meant that if she felt pressured in this way, she would invariably turn to alcohol.

It seems such a simple thing to me. We were both house proud, having been heavily involved with the work done to our homes over the years. Surely anyone can understand that both of us actually felt completely snubbed by Sam's family when their visits became scarce. For me it wasn't a major problem but for her it was extremely important that she felt valued, and more importantly, listened to. It became more and more evident that she wasn't being treated as having parity with her sisters.

There were times when we were invited to Wanda's house and I would try to get out of it. We were often phoned within 24 hours of the event, as though we were a last resort, anyway. It did seem as though we were sometimes only needed to make up the numbers. I would sometimes tell Sam I didn't want to go but she would say we had to. She felt that not going would be worse, as it would allow any resentment to gain further traction, which was fair enough.

Boxing Day each year was always a tricky one for us, as it was invariably held at Wanda's house. This seemed to be accepted by everyone, and was never really contested, although there were a few held at Sandra's.

We did make an attempt one year to have things at our house, but it was met with snide comments about the food from Terry, so we didn't bother trying again.

When at Wanda's house parties, we would all wait in anticipation, to be marshalled into the living room where we would be told when we could all start eating, and when we could all start formally giving out presents. It was all a little too contrived and controlled for me.

The food would usually be good, but there was such a fuss made of it that it would often not be enjoyable. Everyone tended to just eat after being told they could, and then split into separate gangs in different parts of the house.

As the nephews and nieces got older there would be young drinkers together in one clique, and the older drinkers in another. The children would be largely left to their own devices, while Sam and I would try to break into whichever crowd we could, desperately attempting to tag onto their conversations.

There were never any party games or anything very festive to participate in, so it was only really the food that kept the children and ourselves relatively content. It was all much like being gate-crashers at a stranger's wedding reception.

In more recent times, we started to go to my Mum's, either instead of, or as well as Wanda's, on Boxing Day. At least there we felt we could relax more, and it was friendlier, with only a small collection of family and close friends. We would also have a good time playing party games like charades, as many families did at Christmas. The unceremonious nature of this also helped the children have a better time, which is what it was all about. Adults standing around recounting drinking and football stories didn't really do it for any of us to be honest.

When I raised the issue of a lack of visits to our house, at Christmas or any other time, years later with Wanda, she offered two reasons in mitigation.

Firstly, she said that it was our 'bickering' as a couple which had prevented them from visiting us in our own home all those years.

This bickering, as it was referred to, could easily have been confused with our marital banter. I know of many marriages which have only stayed fresh because of a healthy level of good-humoured 'teasing'. You can see couples like this every day when out shopping. I don't deny that there may have been times when this teasing became more intense, though. In the main, this would be at Wanda's parties, when I was flagging under the pressure of Sam's alcohol issues.

As drink could never be avoided at these affairs then I know there were times when I was struggling to hold things together. We would occasionally argue as a result, although this was not usually a major drama for any of the other numerous guests. More often than not, if she was drinking, I would just leave her to it and move to another room in the house where possible. We were never important enough to have disrupted proceedings too much.

Any public behaviour which may have seemed inappropriate could well have been an example of me…

'Loving the woman, but hating the alcoholic',

….which is a common dilemma for anyone living with an addict.

If only my wife's family had understood, or even tried to, rather than coming up with these feeble cover stories for themselves years later.

Perhaps I am wrong about the amount of upset our disagreements caused Sam's family. After all it must have been pretty awful to have stopped her husband, Terry, visiting us and the kids for over 15 years, without him ever explaining why?

I much prefer the other reason Wanda gave for not taking the trouble to see us as a family in our own home, as I found this a much more honest representation of the facts.
Apparently, she said, *'Terry, doesn't do visiting'.*

Dead right, he didn't even visit his own mother. He would have other members of his family bring her to his house for the big events, like she was merely one of his royal subjects!

Chapter 5: Moving Home

'What do we live for, if it is not to make life less difficult for each other?'
George Eliot

Not long after Jack arrived we put our house on the market, hoping to move to a larger one before we grew our family further. This was the early 90's so unfortunately our timing was awful, as the property market in the UK was in freefall. Staying where we were wasn't really an option as, aside from the fact we needed more room, there were some issues with crime in the area. Our claim to fame was that we once had our Mini stolen and returned by the police, twice on the same night. We needed to get away.

In the meantime our second son Daniel James came along. We went with another king for his middle name, aiming high with our ambitions for him, obviously. Jack had a kind of grudging love for his new brother, which often involved sitting on him when no one was looking. Daniel rarely complained about this for some reason.

In selling our house we knew we were going to have a problem in that we were deep into negative equity. This was a massive problem for many people at that time due to the 'boom and bust' journey the property market had taken. Our timing was awful but we needed a bigger house.

We would have to borrow money from my parents temporarily to enable us to repay the mortgage, which was significantly more than we sold the house for. They had agreed to extend their own mortgage, and then we would repay their loan once we secured our new home.

It seemed to be almost immediately after Daniel that we found out we were expecting another baby. The three of them are actually between

19 months and 2 years apart but it did lead to some people referring to Sam as a 'baby machine'.

We took a big risk in buying another property before we had sold our own, so had two houses and two mortgages now. If we couldn't sell our house quickly our financial position would be untenable. What is life though, without taking risks?

Our new house needed a great deal of work to make it habitable. It had previously been rented out for some years, and was very outdated. I believe the main selling point of this house to Sam, by far, was its proximity to her parents, who lived only around 500 yards away. She was obviously viewing things with rose tinted spectacles and expected to be seeing a lot of them. This never panned out that way at all. In fact it could not have been further from the truth.

I began the project to turn the very ropy house into our new home, doing as much of the work as I could myself, to keep the costs down. I had always been quite handy and enjoyed the renovation work. This involved putting the original fireplaces back in, stripping and varnishing floorboards, replacing interior walls, and the bathroom. I also fitted a new kitchen, some of which I made myself.

Luckily we soon had our first offer on our old house, after around four years of it being on the market. This must have been fate, as the buyer knocked on the door rather than approaching the agent, and we agreed a sale very quickly.

Early in 2000 we moved into our new home, which was in quite a state, with Sam heavily pregnant. The house was a building site, with no curtains or carpets, and every room needing urgent work to be usable in any way.

Just as we were about to move in Sam was diagnosed with a serious pregnancy complication called 'placenta previa' and had to be admitted to hospital immediately. It turned out that our latest addition was going to test our metal, and we were told that the pregnancy complication was potentially fatal for both mother and child. Sam was to expect to remain in hospital until the birth, four to six weeks later.

This was far from ideal as I now had the two boys to look after, and a house unfit for purpose. I had to do the best I could to make it as comfortable as possible for when Sam came out of hospital. There was some help from my Dad, who is an electrician, so at least the wiring would be serviceable.

Thankfully our daughter, Abigail Elizabeth, was born in March 2000, having decided to turn around the right way inside her Mum, just in time to be born, without any major problems. We went with the regal theme again for her middle name, in common with her brothers.

Within the first 24 hours of Sam coming out of hospital Wanda phoned to ask if we were going to come to their house to show them the new baby. This set the pattern for how we were dealt with by them, from that point on.

It was a difficult time with lots going on but we coped well initially. Soon after the birth, though, Sam's mental health started to suffer, and she was diagnosed with post-natal depression by her GP. It was around this time that I first started to fully comprehend just how wide the emotional distance was between Sam and her parents. There had been very little contact from them during her time before, during and after hospital and then no significant help or support on offer once she was back at home either.

I think there was just one attempt made by Sam's Mum, to help her with some ironing. As this was not met with the response she expected, probably as a result of her post-natal depression, it didn't ever happen again.

In fact for the next 17 years or so visits from my wife's parents were restricted almost exclusively to Christmas and birthdays. Sam just didn't have the kind of relationship with them that any daughter would hope to have, and there seemed to be no maternal or paternal bond between them, whatsoever.

We did get some practical help, particularly with the school run when Sam was working, but no family visits. It was her Dad who did the school run for us once or twice a week and he rarely came in the house. When he did, he never sat down and would only stand in the hallway or kitchen.

The grandparents did help us with the cost of school uniforms and shoes for many years but, as I have said to them since, I would have gladly swapped all this for some help with Sam when it was most needed. I do believe, very strongly, that my own and my children's lives would have been far less stressful and dangerous, if they had only taken the trouble to speak to their daughter properly, in her own home, as any caring parent should want to do.

There were quite obviously serious unresolved issues from Sam's childhood which had not been discussed meaningfully, between all those involved. She had a difficult relationship with Wanda, who had apparently been something of a bully when she was younger. Sam still struggles with sleep and has to have a light on before she can relax. This stems back to when her sister would try to frighten her by placing things in her bedroom window. She still has nightmares about a toy 'head' which was used in this way to deliberately upset her as a child.

There was another more disturbing event which occurred at the age of seven, when Sam says she was sexually abused by an acquaintance of her father, whilst on his watch.

He was engaging in what I suppose could be described as a little 'entrepreneurial weekend business', with his daughter in tow. This involved assisting a 'spiv' known as 'Tony the Greek' in loading his car with crockery, at the factory where her Dad worked.

While Sam's father disappeared into the warehouse for another selection of 'hot' wares, this opportunist sat her on his knee and gave her money. A sexual assault then took place, which at such a young age, Sam was hardly likely to have fully appreciated the significance of. Her father had no idea this had taken place at the time, but he was told about it years later.

If this was me, then as a father, I would want to know every single detail of this event. Then I would hunt down the offender, or his family if he was dead. Finally, I would want to sit down with my daughter and talk it through with her calmly. None of this has ever happened at all.

Of course I have not ruled out the possibility that this could be a figment of Sam's imagination. I really don't think so though, having heard her talk about it many, many times now. Even if it was imaginary then surely it should have at least been talked about and taken much more seriously by her parents. Otherwise, I feel it is further reinforcing the lack of emotional attachment they have to her.

There were also events from Sam's mid-teenage years onwards when it seems her mother and father had, to all intents and purposes, forgotten they were still parents completely, once Wanda gave them their first grandchild. I was not around so cannot confirm or deny any of this, but have heard Sam talk about it for as long as I have known her. She definitely felt detached from her parents once they became grandparents.

This detachment has been the main focus of all the subsequent meetings she has had with psychiatrists and therapists over many years since.

I have never been what you might call a touchy-feely person myself. I tend to keep my emotions in check, at least visibly, as much as possible, which is not always the right thing to do. This has definitely not come about from a lack of love and care from my own parents though, it's just the way I have turned out.

This stiff upper lip approach can sometimes give people the impression that you are uncaring, which is definitely not the case with me. I think I tend to show my true feelings in other ways, mostly in my actions. Those who really know me completely understand.

Perhaps I can illustrate this with a story from around this time.

Brandon, Wanda's son, was in the army by the early 2000's and it was the time of the Iraq War. We found out that he was soon to see action as a tank driver. Having lived through the previous Gulf War, and been shocked by the coverage of the conflict, I was moved to make some kind of gesture.

I had a Second World War Campaign Medal which had been my Dad's uncle's, who had got through this war relatively unscathed, so I thought I could offer this to Brandon as a lucky charm of sorts.

We were invited to Wanda's house for a kind of farewell do, before he left for his tour of duty, so I thought I would take the medal along and hand it over to him there. All the usual show-business was in evidence at Wanda's house, although admittedly this was perhaps more excusable on this occasion, being the last time anyone would see him for some time.

An opportunity arose for me to speak to Brandon away from the rest of the family and friends, in private outside. I spied my chance and presented him with the medal, but as I started to explain what it was all about I began to choke up, as I tried to speak.

This was my nephew, who I had seen grow up, so I was hit by a groundswell of emotion. He said he wouldn't be able to wear the medal, and I replied that I hadn't expected he could, it was just to hang on to for luck, and he should give it back to me on his safe return.

Thankfully he did return home after what must have been a terrible experience, which I could never hope to appreciate. My medal didn't come back to me though, and I had to send a gentle reminder via Sam, to his parents. The medal was eventually given back almost a year later, unceremoniously handed back to me with nothing much said, and no recognition at all from Wanda or Terry.

In fact, I never heard the medal talked about by any members of my wife's family. Perhaps because I had not done things in their style, so they didn't want to acknowledge it. Praise or reward wasn't what I was looking for, as it wasn't about me at all. I just thought a simple heartfelt thankyou from him, and more importantly, his parents, would have been in order.

I had loaned the medal for all the right reasons, acting as a concerned member of their family but my actions and motives were simply not appreciated. This has been a continuing theme in the time I have known my wife's family.

Our own family life went on and there were no major problems, just the normal pressures associated with children. People do say that when you have toddlers around this is the best time of anyone's lives. I would tend to agree and I did enjoy being a Dad to my three terrors.

They were all mostly well-behaved, as well as entertaining. We didn't often have to rein them in when they were on show. I think this was, in no small part, due to the fact that they were all good sleepers. They still are.

Although, at the time it could seem quite stressful, I would love to be able to go back to those days again. The utter simplicity of looking after small children, compared to the complexities of teenagers is what appeals most to me, I think.

However, bearing in mind the pregnancy complications with Abigail, and the fact that Sam seemed to be able to get pregnant if I just looked at her, we came to the decision that perhaps three was enough. A more reliable, and more permanent method of contraception was in order.

'We' somehow came to the conclusion that I had to have a vasectomy. I can't quite remember how I fell for this one.

I knew nothing about this operation but after speaking to my own doctor he referred me to another local GP, who spent his own quality time doing these, in his own community spirited way, over most weekends.

A meeting was arranged with the doctor concerned beforehand, where I was told all the various potential disasters which could possibly befall me as a result of the surgery. These could involve anything from never being able to feel anything again, to feeling every step on the ground I took. This was due to the proximity of the nerve endings in that particular vicinity, which he would soon be waving his heavily armed fingers around.

One of the most surreal experiences of my life occurred when I walked into operating room on the day of the procedure.

The doctor asked me if I liked 'Dire Straits', which I did think was both an odd question, and an equally odd choice of music, to be playing as accompaniment to the very delicate 'matter in hand', so to speak. 'Sultans of swing' didn't really inspire any confidence in me, as he commenced his attack on my bits.

Whatever anyone tells you about vasectomies my own experience was one of the most unpleasant things I have ever had to endure. The only blessing was that it didn't last too long.

On leaving the room the doctor held out his gloved hand which contained some pieces of me in it. Pushing these narrow tubes of flesh towards me, he said, *'I hope you aren't having spaghetti tonight'*.

Local folklore says that this doctor from hell can be seen riding his horse around his village, like a deranged Ross Poldark, whilst laughing maniacally at the impact he has had on male appendages for miles around.

I spent the next few weeks walking around the house holding a cushion in front of me. My children had just the right height and energy to hit my tender regions full on, which they did with much regularity.

My operation has resulted in a new skill, though. To this day I can forecast the weather if I cup my right testicle. I had no idea that the slip of a scalpel would transform me into a rather uncomfortable barometer for the rest of my life.

Chapter 6: Family Life

'To succeed in life you need three things: a wishbone, a backbone and a funny bone.'
Reba McEntire

Strangely perhaps, we did go on holiday with my wife's parents for many years. This was mostly to do with the practicalities of having small children, and not a great deal of money. We went on static caravan holidays in the UK for around 10 years with them, early each summer to benefit from the better prices available out of season.

The grandparents weren't used as childminders merely to allow us to have a good time ourselves. We would only leave them alone with the children for short periods in the day occasionally. The rest of the time we would all be mostly together, with some time in our own caravans in the evenings.

As a practical arrangement, largely for the benefit of the children, this worked well and we had some good times. My view was always that if the kids were happy then I was happy.

The tension was still there though, and would sometimes show itself in stand-offs between Sam and her Mum. Her father would be drinking much of the time so would be largely oblivious to it all. He would completely fill his car boot with wine from our local supermarket, before setting off from home.

He took so much wine that we could never ask them to take any of our luggage to help us with space in our car, despite there only being the two of them. They had to put their own luggage on the back seats to accommodate the wine stock.

This tells its own story about my wife's family's relationship with alcohol, which I am afraid I cannot believe has not had any influence on her own close alliance with the demon drink.

This aside, the priority for me was that our children had a good time in a very traditional way, on the beach in Devon, Cornwall or Dorset. They all loved the beach, Daniel would charge at top speed towards the sea excitedly before we had time to pick our spot, sending us into a panic. Much like me, he has never been a strong swimmer. He even had to con the instructor recently so that he could do his scuba diving training, during his four week conservation trip to South Africa.

Jack would demand most of my attention, so we would construct boats in the sand, while Daniel and Abigail would make themselves busy together for hours. We would also do the uniquely British thing and even sit on the beach in the pouring rain and sea wind, as it just had to be done. It just wouldn't be a traditional holiday without this.

I love the coast and would really like to be able to retire there, or at least have a holiday home by the sea one day. The sight and sound of waves crashing against the rocks, I find, both calming and yet at the same time immensely invigorating.

To this day we have still never been on holiday as a couple without the children, but I have no regrets about this at all. What's the fun in making sandcastles with your wife anyway?

My favourite picture of Jack, which we presented to him on his 21st birthday, is of him standing on the beach dressed in flippers and a diving mask. All the children had, to all intents and purposes, a very normal, happy childhood.

When the children were a little older, as reward to myself for reaching the magic age of 40, I bought a classic car on a complete whim. This was a 1968 Triumph Vitesse Tristram convertible, which we were to christen 'Vicky'. I wanted to rekindle my interest in classic cars and I saw this as a way of providing me with some respite and escape from reality. It also gave the option of days out with the whole family in the open air.

It had hurt when I had to sell the MX5 when the children came along and wanted the wind in my hair again, while I still had some. The good thing about this car was that it could legally seat the five of us, with no roof, so it was ideal for trips out in the summer. The car only cost me £1,750 so I could justify the expense, despite our somewhat dodgy financial position. There was no road tax to pay, very cheap insurance, and repairs and servicing would be affordable as I could do some of this myself. I saw it as a good long term investment for us.

We did have some good fun in the Triumph with the children. They seemed to relish the thrill of open-air motoring, and the wide-eyed looks we got from people. Many of these probably thought the car was something much better than it was, but who cares. I always tried to keep it looking good so it did attract some admiration.

One time we arranged a day out in the car, as a family, but didn't realise we would have a werewolf with us.

Daniel had a complete wolf's head and matching brown, hairy, top, I can't remember why, he just did, and it was very realistic. He decided to wear the costume for our outing so, without ceremony or drama, he sat in the back of the car. We drove around for some time watching people's reactions at traffic lights, and the many double-takes of passing pedestrians, and other cars. Daniel just sat there in the back seat barely moving, aside from occasionally tilting his wolf-head to one side very slowly, like a curious dog, it was hilarious.

There was also the time when a wheel fell off at some speed on the A50 with all of us in the car. We skidded dramatically to a halt, luckily in a straight line, with the wheel still rolling away behind us, onto the grass verge. After phoning some friends to pick up the children, I then just put the wheel back on and drove home, simples!

I still have Vicky, ten years on, and use her whenever I can during the summer. I can't see me ever selling her, she has captured too many happy memories for me.

Of our children, Daniel was always the more deadpan in his approach to humour. I remember the time when he was around seven or eight and we had a knock at the door, to find some of the neighbours and their children laughing hysterically. They were pointing up at Daniel's bedroom window, so I went out into the drive to look up. There was Daniel, stood on the window-sill inside his room, absolutely stark naked in the shape of a cross, arms outstretched, and with everything he had on show.

'He thinks he's Jesus!' the children in the street were shouting.

Jack also has a good sense of humour but a much more measured, sensitive side to his character. We have lots of photographs of him with his very cheeky smile, usually because he had just got away with doing something to his brother before the picture was taken.

He was quite high maintenance when at school and we often used to have to sit with him for hours cajoling him into doing his homework. Nevertheless, it must have paid off as he was moved into the year above in Primary school. He was one of the youngest in his class but simply wasn't being stretched enough.

We were so proud of him when he performed in the primary school play as The King, in 'Joseph and his Technicolour Dream-coat'. It was talked about by the teachers for some time afterwards, as he had the Elvis impersonation off to a tee.

Abigail would play for hours with Daniel and they were very close when young. They would disappear upstairs and build with Lego together for hours and hours, without falling out. This was the very best toy we ever bought, as Abigail was never really interested in dolls or suchlike, while Daniel would immerse himself in a task and only stop to eat.

As she has got older Abigail has lived up to the stereotypical 'dippy blonde' badge at times, and has often had us all in fits of laughter with her approach to life, and her off-the-wall stories. In some ways I think that having to live with an alcoholic mother, and just deal with it as best they could, has given my children a unique gift, in their ability to be able to see the funny side in virtually anything.

Alcoholism is a progressive illness which gradually attacks the body, and particularly the brain by stealth, over time.

There is a misconception amongst many that alcoholics drink spirits all day long, on a continuous basis. I am sure some do, but in Sam's case she has only ever drunk wine. Most addicts have a substance of choice and hers has always been wine. This means it is her brain that has suffered much more than her liver, as can be the case with spirit drinkers.

Sam has also not always drank daily for sustained periods. In fact she has been more of a binge alcoholic, in that she can go a few weeks without succumbing sometimes, but then relapse into daily drinking again for a time.

This makes her very difficult to deal with as I am always waiting for the next drama to unfold, with no ability to plan any aspect of my life. Even very basic planning like what food to buy can become a trial sometimes, when not knowing what priority eating properly would be taking in her mind.

Sam was a good mother to our children in their early years, into Primary school and beyond, in spite of the slow ramping up of her illness. All of them had a great deal of attention from us both, and I don't believe it is any accident that they all did well at school. We would both read to them every day and they were our whole life, as neither of us had any significantly time consuming hobbies or interests, outside of bringing up our children.

We continued doing much the same things when we had children as we did previously as a couple. We would still go to places we would have gone to before we had them, and didn't change our lives to any great degree to accommodate only their interests. Obviously we did take them to places they enjoyed as well, but we didn't pander to them constantly, or drastically change the way we did things, which I think taught them good manners and behaviour.

We would always eat together, and they ate what we did, there were no separate meals for the children. I think this is the reason they have never been picky eaters, and will try virtually anything.

I do think we had a good approach to parenting in general, which I feel has meant our children have learned more from how we have gelled as a family. We have never seen them as anything of an inconvenience, as I know some people do their children. Although I don't have any regrets about this it has definitely made things harder for me now. I do suffer a little from not having built a life of my own, away from my family responsibilities.

The main issue the children had to deal with in their younger years was their Mum's temper, which was being fuelled by her drinking. Again, I failed to link the two things as family life is difficult at times for most people, and patience was very often stretched. Perhaps it was actually that I was in denial, and so didn't want to admit there was a problem with my wife at all.

I remember one particular incident, when Jack fell off his bike in the street. He was probably around eight, and the bike was brand new. He damaged it slightly, but instead of parental concern for his welfare his Mum flew at him in a rage.

She did what many parents would probably have done in times past and smacked him in the street. Unfortunately, at the time we had some busy-body neighbours who saw all this and chose to report Sam to Social Services.

When I found out I rang the department concerned straight away and angrily told them to come to see me, the children, and their school teachers, if they wanted reassurance that we were good parents. I was furious and took this as an unprovoked attack on me as a father. They wouldn't do as I asked, and merely said that a record would be kept on file for two years, and then destroyed, as long as there was no reoccurrence. Happily, the neighbours moved on before too long and there was no repeat of any similar incident in the street.

People I have told this story to since have said that they would have barely survived such an incident themselves. If they had damaged a new bike like this, they would have fully expected their own parents to have acted in a similar way. They felt their own health too, would have been a lesser concern if a new possession had been damaged.

I suppose this illustrates the difficulty in separating normal family stresses and strains and alcohol fuelled problems. Without knowing the person concerned well enough you just wouldn't know whether this was normal, or alcohol-fuelled, behaviour.

Sam's parents and sisters, to this day, still don't understand any of this as they have not been close enough to the problem to ever find out. I cannot remember the last time any of them have spoken to Sam when she has been completely clear of the effects of alcohol.

I will agree that this kind of distance is not uncommon and would be absolutely fine within most families. We definitely don't all live perfect, Hollywood type existences, where all family members have close, caring relationships. However, in a family which has sought to run away from things, and then cast blame on me for how things have turned out, I feel it is unacceptable for them not to have made much more effort to understand Sam's condition.

I have tried over many years to separate how much of Sam's problem relates to addiction, and how much relates to her underlying character. After talking this through with many people, including specialists in their field, I have concluded that it is much more about the addiction. Alcoholism is such a powerful, life changing thing, and has been part of her for so long, that essentially the addiction 'is' her and she cannot easily be separated from it.

The stigma which still exists around addiction means that there is such a massive amount of 'fake news' and misunderstanding that people can easily forget that addicts are still people. They are still family members who need help as much as anyone who is ill.

How I treated my wife would not have been any different whatever her illness had been. With the exception of recent years, when she became totally unmanageable at times, I have always acted as most good husbands would be expected to. When her drinking was under control we would have a close bond and always sit together in the evening, her legs on mine, on the sofa.

In contrast I have not seen any of my wife's family sit together for any sustained period of time. They have tended to have a 'separate sofa' approach. I very rarely saw any of them sit closely, unless in the case of Wanda, she was on show for the camera, or a room full of people.

I can genuinely never recall any time when Sam's Mum has sat next to her, or even close to her. They were always some distance apart, in many ways.

Our evenings as a couple would largely be spent watching television together, although in the early years Sam did like to read or knit. She was a really fast reader and could complete a book in just one night. She was also a very accomplished knitter and made some of the children's baby and toddler clothes, as well as some for other family members.

One of Sam's best attributes for me, though, was that she was a very accomplished cook. We did go vegetarian for a while, and she managed to come up with some really tasty alternatives to the usual meat and two veg. Food was one of my few vices so this was definitely a big thing for me, the way to a man's heart and all that.

I know I have implied that I was perhaps not the most romantic of husbands but this was not always the case. I remember one example of how I could turn it on when required. There were others but I do recall this one well.

We had been on a day out in Alderley Edge and, as ever, Sam had taken an interest in looking in the windows of jewellery shops. Often the items she admired were way out of our reach, so I would just let her point them out and feign interest. This time, though, amongst the many on display was an eternity ring which I could tell she liked, and most importantly, wasn't massively expensive. We returned home without any purchases though, which was usually the case.

I was working in the depths of the West Midlands at that time but the next day I spied my chance and drove the 160 mile round trip, in work time, to buy the ring Sam had been admiring. Understandably, this went down really well and she still wears the ring every day, just about.

If only I could have foreseen that Sam would be pawning this prized possession to fund her drinking, on a regular basis in years to come.

I think I have now bought it back for her from pawn shops on three separate occasions, along with her engagement ring, wedding ring and other jewellery with sentimental attachment.

Addiction knows no boundaries.

Chapter 7: On to High School

'Tough times never last. Tough people do.'
Robert Schuller

When Jack reached decision time for high school I was very keen to ensure we gave him the very best chance we could in life. He was very intelligent, but high maintenance, so we took him to see the best two schools we could find, one selective and one not. After sucking in the atmosphere of both establishments he chose the selective school. He had bought into the feel of the place when he looked around it. There was no specific overriding reason he could offer but he had obviously made up his mind.

Children can be very perceptive and I think Jack could see that this school was far from being just about good discipline and results alone, and had a lot more than this to offer him. It was the furthest away from home, and with no school bus service, but that was much less important to us than the quality of the all-round education.

He subsequently passed the entrance test, and seemed pleased with his decision. We were so proud of him, as he was the only boy from his primary school to go there, so Jack had to leave his friends behind.

All this appeared to cause some upset with Sam's Mum who I feel had planned for Jack to follow his cousins' path through the other high school. All six of my wife's sisters' children had gone to this one, so we had rocked the boat somewhat. I was at pains to explain to my mother-in-law at the time, and since, that it was a choice made primarily for our son, but I don't think she ever really understood this.

Not long after Jack commenced high school the Local Authority announced plans for its closure under the flawed, 'Building Schools for the Future' program. It was being used as a local political football to further some individuals' careers, rather than being anything to do with improving education in the area.

I immediately joined the campaign to fight this closure and helped on the 'Parents Action Group'. We lobbied MP's, staged meetings with parents, and pestered the local authority continually, to help force a reconsideration. After a prolonged battle the decision makers came to their senses, and thankfully the school was saved. My own interest in education had been re-ignited.

I put myself forward for election as a parent governor in 2009, was voted in and appointed, and have served on the Governing Body at the school since then. I have been re-elected for three terms of office now, by parental ballot. The parents seem to continue to appreciate my straight-talking honesty.

Having this second, unpaid job was a welcome distraction from the trials at home, and I feel it is one of the things that has helped me stay sane over the years. When times were really tough I have been able to use my knowledge and experience to add some value, which has helped with my own morale when times were hard.

In a similar vein, all I ever wanted from my own and my wife's family was a degree of respect. I never achieved this from the out-laws. For some reason my brothers-in-law were always the go to men in the family, certainly not me, unless there was some menial practical task which I was needed for.

At Daniel's school, around 18 months before he was due to leave for high school, there was a mass exodus of teaching staff. Knowing the school quite well, we had serious misgivings about its ability to cope with this, so felt we had to do our best to ensure his education was not adversely affected.

As things were going well for me at work at the time we decided to remove both Daniel and Abigail and pay for them to go to a private primary school. We had lost some faith in state Primaries and didn't want our children to become victims of the system. This was a big commitment for us financially but seemed just about affordable at the time. I thought my children's education was far too important to be allowed to suffer, so we took the risk.

Daniel was a very difficult character to understand at times, and we were worried that if the quality of his teaching suffered he may not realise his full potential.

What I didn't know at the time was that we were on the verge of the worldwide banking crisis. The ensuing economic meltdown this caused meant that my job in financial services was hit really hard. My pay reduced drastically overnight and we were left with substantial debts to maintain. I took such a huge drop in pay that it meant the whole cost of the private schooling instantly became an additional loan.

Abigail would have to change schools again whilst Daniel could just about see out his time at the private school, before going on to the same selective, state high school as his brother.

I have never regretted spending the money on private education, even though it was short lived and created more debt. Daniel still has friends from this spell today and I actually regard his time in this school as invaluable to his future academic development. It gave him exactly the boost he needed to focus his attention on learning.

He now studies Biology at Lancaster University and Jack, after taking a working break, studies History at Derby.

It was around this time that Sam's condition took a very serious turn for the worse. As well as drinking she was going through a bad time with the menopause, very early at the age of around 40. The physical aspects of this, including the volatile hormonal issues, were playing havoc with her overall mental health. As previously, she was using alcohol as self-medication for her anxiety and depression.

On New Year's Eve 2008, after drinking heavily over the Christmas period, as well as suffering from severe blood loss, Sam was taken ill. She didn't look well at all and had to go to bed.

During the early hours of New Year's Day, whilst lying next to me in bed, she began to convulse uncontrollably. It was one of the scariest things I have ever witnessed. Her whole body shook, as did the bed, and she let out a very strange moaning noise, much like a wild animal in pain. Once this very explosive fit subsided she seemed to have absolutely no idea where she was, and was completely disorientated.

I called for an ambulance and went with Sam to hospital. Almost immediately after lying down in a hospital bed a second seizure hit her, and she had to be forcibly held still by a doctor and three nurses. This time the convulsions seemed to last forever, and I felt as though I was watching one of those television hospital dramas, yet was very much part of the story this time.

To see my wife in this sort of terrible state was horrendous and I think I simply went into a kind of automatic mode. I accepted everything that was happening, and everything that was said to me by the consultants and nurses, in a very pragmatic way, and in something of a daze.

The consultant later showed me Sam's brain scan picture, alongside that of a normal one, to illustrate how hers had been shrunk by the effects of alcohol over the many years she had been drinking. He told me this was irreversible, and would affect her cognitive ability for the rest of her life.

Sam struggled to recognise me at all as she gradually began to regain her senses in hospital. Eventually she seemed to be returning to normal but was indignant, and said she didn't want to stay there. I convinced her it was in her best interests to stay in the care of the nurses and left, once she seemed settled, to the sound of some whispering from some of the staff, scoffing about alcohol.

Events took a strange turn when, instead of waiting to be discharged, Sam left the ward without informing anyone. The first I knew of this was when she turned up at home in a taxi, still in her dressing gown.

She had simply walked out of the hospital and got around a mile away, in her slippers, before flagging down the taxi. I imagine the driver must have thought she had been to a New Year fancy dress party. My complaints to the hospital afterwards fell on deaf ears. They seemed to dismiss the fact that a patient who had almost died, could just walk out of the entrance in her nightwear, without being challenged at all on the way.

It seems that the seizures were brought about by alcohol starvation, and a general lack of blood, following her severe menstrual bleeding relating to the menopause. This, combined with the fact she had been too ill to eat or drink properly, after the inevitable high volumes over Christmas, had caused her body to react in this very violent way. It could all have very easily ended her life.

I asked Sandra's husband, Sean, to take all the wine away which we had bought in for Christmas and New Year. This was the last time I ever bought alcohol for the house. I stopped drinking almost completely myself from that point on. The only time I ever drink now is very much in moderation when out, which isn't very often at all.

The problem with this approach, though, was that Steph reverted back to more secret drinking, but I think this would have happened anyway, as it had in the past. It is simply part of her condition.

We never had any money offered for all the wine which was taken away, I probably would have refused but it would have been nice to have been asked. There was a car boot full as I had bought a stock for ourselves and possible guests over Christmas and this hadn't happened.

I can only recall one visit from Sam's parents after she returned from hospital following the seizures. In fact this may have been the last time they ever came to our house as a couple, outside of birthdays and Christmas, which was of course primarily for the children. We did always have them for Christmas dinner on alternate years back then.

Once Sam was on the mend it seemed that her brush with death had been a massive wake-up call for her. In a similar way to a re-booted computer she took on a whole new attitude, and seemed like a brand new person, with new vigour and resolve. She engaged with some local alcohol support from an organisation called Aquarius. I don't think this was the main reason she stopped, but the important thing was that she did stop drinking, and managed to maintain this.

When speaking to these well-meaning alcohol support counsellors, Sam was always told that she shouldn't be there. They were obviously more used to dealing with the less capable, more hopeless members of society, shall we say. This was an ever-present problem and, because of the way she conducted herself in the meetings, they could sometimes not give her much attention. They would not be able to see through the intelligence to the very serious underlying strength of her addiction.

I have found this is an issue with alcohol treatment generally, in that all alcoholics are different, but assumptions are often made simply because there is not the level of expertise or feet on the ground to cope with the high numbers of clients. Many of the counsellors Sam saw were quite young so they just couldn't relate to her well, as a middle-aged, intelligent woman.

Anyway, she did stop, which was the main thing, and then decided straight away that she would retrain as a Teaching Assistant.

She had received medical severance from her previous role with Royal Mail. Her employer had instigated medical assessments of her anxiety and depression after a long period of sick leave. They had concluded, as a result of these, that the role she would have to embrace in their new call centre was not suitable for her state of health. Sam received a small cash pay-off for ending her 20 year plus career with them. It was a shame as only a few years before she had been very close to gaining a management role, but this was now not to be.

The plus side to all this was that Sam now had an opportunity to take up her own lifelong interest in education. She had been volunteering at the children's school and was very much enjoying working there.

She had now lost her driving licence due to the seizures so had to walk or use public transport to attend her courses and training placements. To regain her licence she would have to re-apply every 12 months and supply medical information. It was the possibility of her suffering another fit which driver licensing were most worried about.

They did seem to make the whole process as difficult and long-winded as possible, understandably perhaps, but she had never been caught drink-driving, yet these people seemed to get their licences back relatively quickly, and without a great deal of trouble.

Despite these difficulties Sam completed her Teaching Assistant qualification with flying colours. She put a huge amount of work into the course, and seemed to relish it. Her tutor said it was the best work he had seen in years, and to a much higher standard than required.

It was soon after qualifying that Sam gained a part-time job, followed by a full-time one in a local primary school. She had always wanted to go into teaching and this could be her route into this career. I knew she had the ability, as I had seen her work with our own children.

Sam stayed sober for the next couple of years and family life returned to a degree of normality. We were both now working again and gradually rebuilding our finances.

Things were starting to feel much more positive.

Then out of the blue, for some unexplained reason, which I will never understand, the old enemy returned.

Chapter 8: Distances Increase

'A problem is a chance for you to do your best.'
Duke Ellington

I didn't want to believe the drinking had re-started so tried to carry on as though nothing had happened. I was still working in the West Midlands for much of this time so would usually be quite late getting home in the evening.

Often I would hear shouting from the house as I pulled into the drive. Steph would be either verbally attacking the children or swaying gently back and forth at the cooker, like a tree in the wind, in an attempt to prepare a meal.

A recognised symptom of Sam's depression and addiction is the inability to complete tasks, so I have spent many years finishing meals, hanging up wet washing, and tidying up after abandoned cleaning efforts. Coming in from work would mean me regularly having to rescue food and trying to calm the situation down in the house, with limited success.

I began to see my job as an escape rather than a necessity and was not in any rush to come home, knowing that there would be the usual nightmare to deal with. I would use some of my work colleagues as very cheap counsellors, by offloading my problems onto them.
This did actually help me get through it all and I learned to make light of things and laugh about my life, even though it was enduring a shockingly bad existence really.

I am still friends with some of the people I worked with around this time and we meet a few times a year, even though we live miles away from each other. I think they have genuinely been concerned about

my wellbeing all these years, having heard what I was having to put up with on a daily basis, and the effect it was having on me.
Sam's emotional distance from her parents, which was outrageous when you consider they lived so close by, continued with no improvement. It was left to me to try to explain to them about their daughter's deterioration in health, when I was called on for errands or odd-jobs at their house.

It was around this time that my mother-in-law started to refer to me, in company, as *'favourite son-in-law'*. I think this may have been a kind of deflecting tactic, as she knew very well what was going on with Sam, and the stress I was under, I had told her often enough. I think it was also driven by her guilt at how she had taken no interest in her daughter's health and welfare at all, and left it to me alone.

Whilst putting up guttering, fixing light fittings and doing various other minor repairs at their house I would give them the updates on Sam, in the hope that they would do something to help. I soon realised I was attempting to move the absolute immoveable.

They had no intention whatsoever of even taking the trouble to simply talk to their daughter one-to-one. Talking would only ever happen at the big family events, where conversation in the true sense of the word never happened, only shallow chit-chat. This was also the case with Sam's sisters who rarely took the trouble to talk to her face to face, as family members should be able to, especially when they all knew she was unwell.

I do feel that this lack of contact inflamed Sam's illness as it increased the detachment she felt from her family. It also provided all the ammunition her addiction needed, by fuelling increasing bitterness.

Life was getting really difficult for me now, and I seized on an opportunity to speak to Sandra about everything. As a result of this, she and Sean suggested that Sam stay with them for a while, so she spent a couple of weeks at Sandra's house, sometime in early 2014.

Sam was working at this time and had not yet descended into the next phase of her addiction. Her behaviour was manageable, although she did continue to drink upstairs in secret during her stay with her sister and brother-in-law, while they openly drank downstairs.

She also spent a couple of nights at Wanda's house sometime after this and was accused of drinking their……Calvados!

Their house was very much like a liquor store so it isn't surprising that she would have found something to drink. The fact that what she did find was an expensive, and very pretentious, apple liqueur seemed much more important to Wanda than the real problem.

Sam did tell me that Wanda and her husband also continued to drink themselves, while she was there. They made no real attempt to hide the fact apparently, very thoughtful and considerate of them. I suppose it further reinforces the total lack of will to empathise in any way with Sam or me. It was all only an unfortunate inconvenience to them, with no real thought for what may actually be happening.

I have been told by people in the know that the Police have one of the highest incidences of alcoholism of any profession, so I would not be at all surprised if Wanda should become one of those statistics one day. She certainly didn't seem to recognise the link between Sam's addiction and her own regular, and often excessive, drinking at all.

After years of dealing with this things began to get worse. Sam took on a more abusive, violent persona when under the influence and became totally unstable for long periods. It was becoming ever more difficult to maintain any level of normality for me and the kids.

We took a joint, considered decision later that year that, as the children had important exams looming, she would move out of our home temporarily and rent a flat.

The plan was that she would use the time to get her head together and hopefully return to the family home after six months with renewed energy, and most importantly, sobriety. She assured us all that she had stopped drinking before, so would do it again.

Things did not go to plan at all and Sam's parents and sisters removed themselves from her life still further. I had hoped that the opposite would happen, and they would all support her with her move, as well as visit her to offer whatever help they could.

She actually had just one, very reluctant, visit from her parents, one from Sandra, and two from Wanda, in the whole of the time she was in the flat. She tells me her father never un-crossed his arms for the whole time he was there. The two visits from Wanda were both when she was on duty as a Police Officer and in full uniform. The first of these involved her telling Sam to be quiet so she could answer her police radio. On the second one she brought her own takeaway coffee with her, and none for Sam. Fantastic body language and rapport building!

Wanda often used her job as the reason she wasn't able to help Sam, me or the children. I did try to point out to her that most of us worked a similar number of hours, and it was how she used her own time away from her job which really mattered. Surely we were family weren't we?

Truth be told, I don't think Wanda ever regarded us as being worthy of any of her own free time, she did use the single word answer, *'priorities'* when I asked her the reason for this once, which I suppose sums things up well.

The rest of Sam's time in the flat, having not lived alone for over 20 years, was spent without any visitors at all, so it was left to me to call. During this period she continued to drink, and drive, having had her licence returned under annual review.
I found it very difficult to come to terms with the way Sam's family were behaving. We had never had any arguments in all the time I had known them and, as far as I knew, I hadn't done anything which could cause any serious ill-feeling. Despite this they were becoming ever more distant and isolating me and the children more and more. Nobody was making any effort to speak to me to ask how I was coping, or much, much, much more importantly, how the children were doing.

On the run up to her going into the flat Steph had a little practical help from Sandra. She helped her look for a good rental property and loaned her a fridge, which Sean dropped off for her. They also gave her the first two months' rent, which I have now fully repaid to them. Wanda sourced Sam a microwave for her time at the flat. She made a point of asking for the instruction manual back as soon as I returned it to her at the end of the rental.

I went to Sandra's house a number of times and chatted about the situation with her and her husband. We had always got on better than I had with Wanda and Terry. I had even very occasionally had proper conversations, outside of the usual mass gatherings, so I thought it was worth a try. When I went to their house to talk about the problems I was having with Sam though, they would never entertain discussing anything to do with Sam's parents.

Sandra would say that their abandonment of their daughter was only my *'opinion'*. She used this phrase more than once and it has rung in my head ever since. Based on everything that had happened it could hardly be described as being just an opinion, could it!?

However, we didn't argue about this and I honestly thought they would be supportive of Sam. Once she was in the flat though, every member of Sam's family acted as though she had left the country. In fact, she had only moved a few miles from home. It was just off the main bus route into the city centre, so her mother would have passed close by most days.

The situation became untenable for Sam when, after a few months in the flat, she lost her job, when she was reported by another member of staff for being under the influence in work time. I helped her to fight a prolonged battle with her employers, who had not followed the correct procedures for dealing with such cases. Sam had been under treatment for her mental health problems, which they were fully aware of at the time. They had a policy in such cases which they chose to completely ignore.

Sam's dismissal was only allowed to happen due to our inability to raise the money for an employment tribunal. The law has now been changed on this, but unfortunately too late for Sam. She lost her job, never to work in the profession again I expect.

We had some welcome help at this time from her uncle who was the only member of the family to show any real understanding of Sam's illness. I asked him if he would be Sam's representative at her appeal hearing, as the Union representative was quite obviously in the pockets of the Local Authority. He had turned up for the disciplinary hearings in the same car as the HR representative, which was ludicrous.

I believe that one of the reasons Sam's uncle may have wanted to help was that, as he told me some time later, he had almost fallen into addiction himself for a short time while working abroad, in his younger days.

He was actually Sam's Mum's twin brother but you would never have guessed. He has no children of his own, but has shown more care and compassion towards Sam, and me, than any other members of her family have.

I began to lose patience with my wife's family and started to send letters and emails, after having one last attempt to get a reaction face to face from her parents, without success. They just didn't seem to want to even try to accept the problem at all. In the complete absence of any visits from them, and the great difficulty I had in using the phone at home in front of Sam, emails between me and her sisters became the only effective way to communicate. I could send these while on breaks at work, and say what I thought I needed to, without being interrupted or overheard.

There were several bouts of email tennis, mostly between me and Wanda, which became angrier on both sides. Unlike my sister-in-law though, I did not resort to name-calling, only some undeniable home-truths.

Despite my aim being to get some level of support for us nothing changed at all in terms of meaningful contact. My wife's family were simply running away and hiding.

The responses to my written pleas were somewhat worse than I ever would have expected in the circumstances. There was no allowance whatsoever made for my own state of mind, and the immense pressure I was under. The main culprits were Wanda and Terry.

He also told me, face-to-face, that Sam was wholly my own responsibility, being married to her, and that my own mother should be the one to help us, not Sam's. He said this with Wanda standing between him and me, as his bodyguard. This illustrated the calibre of the man very well.

The perverse defence of Sam's parents by all members of her family had actually been happening for as long as I had known them. For some reason their other daughters, and their husbands, and even their children, all felt that they had to be protected from any involvement with life's many problems and dilemmas, at all costs.

I had been told that my mother-in-law was 'dying' for the first time many years ago, when Jack was a baby. It was around the time Sam was first diagnosed with post-natal depression, and it looked as though her parents may be needed. They were not a great deal older than I am now.

Sam can actually pinpoint the very day and circumstances when she was told personally, by Sandra. I can't be quite as specific but am in no doubt that this has been a running theme all these years. Both of us have had it brought up whenever there was any, even mildly contentious, issue raised.

The big excuse card had been played for the first time all these years ago, but it was definitely not the last. The imminent death threat was always the protective response from both sisters when anything at all maternal, paternal, or even simply responsible, was expected of Sam's parents. They were either dying or too old, or too retired. I found this impossible to comprehend.

At the time of writing Sam's mother is still very much alive, goes out shopping in the city centre most days and has several holidays each year. She seems to be suffering one of the longest waits on death row I have heard of.

Wanda told me when we last spoke, a while ago now, that my mother-in-law was starting to lose her memory. Well she still finds her way to the bus stop, and even the South West coast in their own car, without much trouble, so she is doing ok as far as I can tell.

I think perhaps she may have lost some memory skills many, many years ago though, when she seems to have forgotten she had a daughter.

In any case, there is no amount of age or infirmity which should be able to diminish the love of a mother for her own child, is there, surely?

Chapter 9: Home Again

'Success and failure are greatly overrated but failure gives you a whole lot more to talk about.'
<u>Hildegard Knef</u>

Sam came home from the flat and we picked up where we left off, but with much more debt following the expense of the rental. As ever, she had been unable to control her spending at all, so there were substantial bills to be settled.

Things began to get even worse when she returned. I think she had expected to come back to the same place and people she had left behind, but it wasn't that simple. We had become accustomed to living without her, as a unit, and the stability this had given me and the children was going to be difficult to give up.

I probably compounded things by not agreeing to sleep in the same bed when she first came back home. The reason for this was that I knew if I acted like everything was fine it would give her licence to return to her old ways.

In truth, whatever I had done would not have affected this, as she would drink no matter what the sleeping arrangements were. She would say that sleeping together as a couple in the same bed, as we always had, would help her to stay sober. In fact what would actually happen was that within a day or two of me backing down to her demands to share a bed, she would relapse, so there really was no benefit to be had.

My own standpoint was that if I was sleeping with her then I was, in effect, condoning her behaviour. For this reason I would be furious if I found that she had lied to me and drank, when sharing a bed with me.

The truth was, no matter what I tried to do, and what behaviour I attempted to change, there was no point. The power of Sam's addiction was just far too strong for either of us to compete with.

Her persona when drunk developed into an even more aggressive, abusive, and now also violent, monster. She would attack me and Abigail, in particular, both mentally and physically, and we had no way to deal with it, and nobody we could call on for help.

Daniel was more able to shut himself away from much of the conflict. When he did get involved, by necessity, he would not hold back in how he dealt with his Mum. This meant that I would sometimes use him as a threat, if he was around. Sam would usually not want to risk upsetting Daniel as she knew he would give her no quarter. I would tell her to calm down or I would get him involved, which she would never want to happen.

Jack was less exposed to his Mum's aggression than the rest of us as he was either working or with his girlfriend most of the time. I suppose this was a blessing in some ways, as I don't know quite how he would have lived with what we were having to on a daily basis.

I took the decision early on that I would not involve my own parents directly with Sam when she was in this state, as she was not their daughter or sister. They offered enough help and support in other ways, in terms of practical and emotional support for us all.

Wanda once told me that the reason my wife's parents couldn't help us was a *'generational'* issue. Well my own parents were not far behind them in age, although admittedly they had probably been the right age to fully espouse the more open era of the 1960's. The generation defence doesn't wash with me at all though. Alcoholism is far from being only a recent plague to hit the planet. It has been around for as long as we have had the ability to make the various toxic liquids. Families have had to cope with addiction for centuries.

The Bronte sisters, along with their father, looked after their alcoholic brother, at home with them, until his death. This was the early 19th century yet it didn't stop them seeing that this was a member of their family, who was ILL. They also managed to knock out the odd classic novel along the way.

The fact is there is no mitigation for not acting as a parent or sibling should, particularly when a member of the family is sick. No matter what generation you are from. It's totally irrelevant.

When she wasn't drinking Sam was still very much a wife and mother. Anyone meeting her between her episodes would not think there was anything wrong at all. She seemed to be able to switch into another gear when she really needed to. She had lost a great deal of weight though, and it didn't suit her at all. She looked drained, and older than her years. She didn't look after herself in the same way she used to, and seemed to care less about the way she dressed.

As ever though, she was very accomplished at giving the impression of normality, especially to people she had only just met. This created problems of its own, in that whenever she was trying to get help with her addiction or mental health, those assessing had great difficulty categorising her.

Essentially, Sam was far too clever for her own good, or the good of her husband and children.

She has actually always had a great deal of insecurity about her own level of intelligence, and has often accused me of doing this down, which I don't. I know that she was easily capable of going to university, but it's her parents who obviously thought otherwise. This is undoubtedly where some of Sam's feelings of low self-worth originated from. She wanted to continue in education but a decision was made for her, which knocked this on the head completely.

The other issue we had with Sam, which still persists today, is that it is almost impossible to get treatment for a mental health problem if alcohol is involved. When you consider that many people suffering with poor mental health will self-medicate with alcohol, this becomes a huge ongoing frustration.

Sam simply had to stop drinking altogether, and then sustain this for long enough to get the attention she needed to address her longstanding anxiety and depression.

She would be prescribed anti-depressants from time to time by her GP, but these would never be allowed to stabilise, and so would not work effectively. She would drink while taking them, so the drugs were not being allowed to do what they should. On top of this her brain would be sent into complete disarray, along with her sleeping patterns and behaviours, by the unhealthy combination of drugs and alcohol. This was the vicious circle we were trapped in, and still are.

When drifting in and out of her passages of insanity Sam would continually ask me if I still loved her. Like many men I had always struggled with the 'L' word. I had never found it easy to say, but after being badgered I would eventually give in. She seemed to constantly need reassurance that I still loved her, which was understandable for many reasons I suppose.

Firstly, I believe she did recognise at least some of what she was subjecting us all to during her drink fuelled rampages. I would have to remind her of the true extent of what she had said and done though, and I don't think she ever really fully understood the hurt these caused.

Secondly, the more she came to realise that I was absolutely all she had in the world, the more she seemed to want to reassure herself that I was still there for her.

I would try to explain to her that, yes, I still loved her, but I detested the alcoholic, as we all did. To me, the two entities were so far apart that they could not possibly be thought of as the same person. In the longer spells of sobriety she would seem to take all this on board and appreciate, at least partially, what she was putting me and the children through.

I would tell her that she shouldn't need any further proof of my commitment, when I was still here by her side. There was nothing more I could do. Remorse and humility never really surfaced very often though, and I found this particularly difficult to deal with. She would expect us all to treat her as though absolutely nothing had happened, after each of her bouts of abuse.

All this created a huge disparity in our family dynamic. One day everything could be absolutely fine, with us all getting on. The next day we would be in a totally different place, so very different that it was beyond comprehension.

I continued to attempt to explain the situation by email to Wanda and Sandra. I rarely got any response at all from Sandra who at one point actually said that she didn't like to read or send emails, and preferred to speak face to face. I imagine a teacher who didn't like to read would present a problem to her pupils, and the school she worked at. As for the face to face aspect, there was no attempt made to talk things through with me, so I can't think how she was going to achieve this.

As for Wanda, her responses to my emails largely consisted of various forms of denial, mistruths, and terms of derision, as well as showing a total disrespect for my intentions towards her sister. At one point she even referred to Sam's previous boyfriends, telling me she had been much happier with them than with me. Thanks a bunch!

Sam would occasionally phone her sisters when under the influence, in fact it was now the only time she would speak to them. The effects of her total abandonment meant she just couldn't bring herself to attempt any contact when she was sober, as it was too upsetting for her. They certainly never phoned her, or me, when she was completely calm and stable.

I explained to both sisters that it was not only pointless, but also potentially damaging to me and the children, for them to allow a drink-fuelled phone-call to continue. They were never around for the aftermath, we were.

My advice to them was to politely end the call and arrange with me to meet to discuss things as much as they liked, in a much more coherent, lucid way. In our own home, where Sam would feel more comfortable. I was the only one who would know when Sam was in the right state of mind to see them, so sorting this out with me was the only logical, sensible way to help at all.

They obviously didn't agree, continued to ignore me, and then would get drawn into arguments with an alcoholic by phone, which was frankly pathetic.

I have learned from organisations such as Al-anon that the phone-calls Sam was making were what they refer to as.

'The Alcoholic's Weapons'.

'The addict is projecting an image of self-hatred against the other person. The reaction they get then justifies previous drinking, and offers them an additional excuse to drink more'.

Perhaps only those closest to an alcoholic would truly be able to understand this, however there was never any attempt to do so by my wife's parents or sisters. They carried on ignoring and deriding me, whilst using the inebriated phone-calls from Steph as a way to justify their own complete separation from us all.

There were two adults and three children all suffering a truly awful time yet none of my wife's family were prepared to listen to me or, dare I say it, take the initiative themselves and do something to help us. There really wasn't anything complicated required at all. They merely had to talk to me, talk to my wife when sober, talk to my children, in our own home with a cup of tea and their coats removed.

'Alcoholism is the disease that makes you too selfish to see the havoc you have created, and care about the people you shattered'.

I do think this also applies to my wife's family, who have been no less selfish in their approach to the illness themselves. Particularly in how they have chosen to deal with all those directly affected by it.

We all project an image of our true selves in the way we interact with other people, and society as a whole. I believe that success in life is absolutely nothing to do with material gain, possessions and careers.

The real test of success in life is how you will be remembered, and most importantly, the emotional legacy you leave your family.

Chapter 10: A Knock on the Door

'Learn from yesterday, live for today, hope for tomorrow. The important thing is not to stop questioning.'
Albert Einstein

Around this time there was another massive event which would impact heavily on us all. Very early one morning I was woken by a loud knock on the door.

When I had thrown on my dressing gown and dashed downstairs I opened the door to find two paramedics stood there. My first reaction was that they had come to the wrong house, so I just stood motionless, and didn't let them in. When I asked what this was all about they said they had received a call about someone taking an overdose.

Confused and panicked, I rushed back upstairs and burst into Abigail's bedroom. I knew instantly from the look on her face that it was her who had taken the overdose.

It turned out she had taken a substantial amount of paracetamol tablets and other painkillers.

Her Mum had been drinking so I gave her short shrift and went with Abigail in the ambulance to the hospital. I spent most of that day there with her, watching her vomit continually, while I held her hair out of the way and tried to keep her calm. It was one of the scariest times of my life, to see my daughter in this mess.

The fear of not knowing if the antidote would work was horrific, and the consultant was vague enough with his answers to my questions not to quell my concerns. I began to feel guilt ridden, had I caused this? Was I to blame for sticking with her mother? Could I have done something differently?

Abigail was kept in hospital for a few days until she was given the all clear. She was kept on an antidote and saline drip for the whole of this time, as the concentration of the paracetamol in her small body was very high. The consultant told her that he had seen people die as a result of paracetamol overdoses and it was a horrible, and very painful death. Their internal organs would be turned to mush, and there was no way of arresting this once the damage was done.

Once Abigail felt up to it, her Mum came to visit her in hospital. She seemed to be remorseful, so I did think perhaps this would have the right effect on her behaviour. I hoped it would be a wake-up call, and that she would realise the very dangerous impact she was having on her own daughter.

When Abigail was subsequently referred for therapy it turned out that, unsurprisingly, her Mum and the whole home situation was by far the biggest problem. She was having other issues as well, as many girls her age did, with her friends, and all sorts of other teenage malaise. There was also a girl she had been involved with on the internet, who had not helped things. This girl had some very serious mental health problems of her own, and had been speaking to Abigail prior to her overdose. It was her who had phoned the ambulance when she realised what had happened.

I felt equally angry and thankful towards this unknown girl. At least she had the sense to phone an ambulance, things could have been very much worse otherwise.

My wife's sister's reaction to all this was unbelievable. After rarely making an appearance at all previously, Wanda turned up at our house on Abigail's release from hospital. She laid into her straight away, accusing her of *'attention seeking'*, before she had even had time to put her hospital bags down.

The incredible irony of Wanda, of all people, making such an accusation did not escape me. I was incandescent and, despite letting things ride in front of Abigail, made my feelings clear to Wanda afterwards. Who was she to have made such an accusation? She didn't know my daughter, she didn't know me. How dare she?!

She did send an apology of sorts in the post to Abigail afterwards, but it still contained a side-swipe at us.

After a period of therapy with CAMHS and Younger Minds, Abigail seemed to be fine and was doing well at school, but sometime after being signed off she took another overdose, out of the blue. This time she did tell me sooner, rather than me finding out from a knock at the door. It didn't make it any less shocking though.

This overdose was even more to do with her Mum's behaviour alone and I knew that something different had to be done. I couldn't allow Sam's addiction to potentially be responsible for killing our daughter.

Once Abigail was back on track and attending therapy I began to make enquiries about residential rehab for Sam. I had made some tentative approaches previously but I knew I now needed to find out exactly how I could go about securing the treatment.

When I discussed everything with Abigail she always said she didn't want to lose her Mum, but found it really difficult to deal with her, as we all did, when she was the ogre she became when she drank. They actually got on well in the periods of sustained sobriety and stability. I even talked to Abigail about whether she thought I should divorce her Mum and she would say she didn't want to lose the house, and have to move away from her friends in our street. She would sometimes call on the friends she had locally for support when she was having difficulty coping with her Mum. I wasn't always the best person to help at these times, so didn't want to disrupt her own support network at all.

When I talked to Abigail's therapists they would say that at times she seemed very strong but other times her mood would drop significantly. They talked about ways for both of us to identify, and help with the low moods, and she was to continue with the sessions until they felt she was strong enough to be signed off again.

I was constantly worrying about what she may do next but at the same time, when we spoke, she would seem quite stable, and was getting on well with her friends from home and school.

There were several meetings at Abigail's school and they kept an eye on her for me. I knew the Head, and the pastoral team, as a governor, so had no qualms about telling them the whole story. I would get regular updates from my eyes and ears in the school as to how she was doing. There didn't seem to be any problems with her work, and she had a good social network around her. Some of these people knew about her overdoses and her Mum's illness, some didn't.

This gave me some comfort, but I was always on edge and would sometimes react irrationally. Trying to manage a teenager by text when she was not at home, whilst remaining calm, was often a trial. I had to allow her some freedom to do what she needed to for her own stability, knowing that this would sometimes mean she would need to stay away from home at her friends' houses. This was a double whammy for me though. I would be just as concerned about where she may be, and what she was up to, as I would be when she was having to suffer her Mum at her worst times.

Abigail actually showed herself to be very sensible. She would take herself away when she needed to, for her own safety, and stay around when things were going well with her Mum. Treating Sam with a degree of contempt when she was under the influence, but as a wife and mother when she was sober, was something we both did consciously. There wasn't really another approach I felt we could adopt.

I hounded the alcohol support bodies concerned to try to get Sam into rehab. I thought that if only I could get her in there would at least be the chance of a recovery. It was a very difficult process though, on two fronts.

Firstly, the BAC O'Connor Centre would only take addicts who they alone felt were committed enough to their process. Sam would also have to agree to undertake a detox week prior to admission, managed at home, and with no help from them at all.

Secondly, the funding would have to be agreed by another Local Authority as we didn't live in the one where the centre was located. We didn't have the money to pay privately for the care, so had to await a decision from them on the funding.

I pushed and pushed whoever I thought had any leverage on the decision. I would question every answer, every policy, and every fob-off, but often it seemed I was just continually banging my head against a really solid brick wall. The bottom line was that until the organisations concerned were utterly convinced that Sam 'wanted' to stop drinking they would not be prepared to step in. I carried on questioning and badgering anyone I thought could possibly help.

Wanda later claimed that she had somehow had some influence over Sam's admission to rehab. I put this to the assessor at the BAC who straight away said this was utter bullshit, and it was also later confirmed to us both.

The fact is that all admissions had to come through their own assessor alone, and were based solely on her own impressions of the client concerned, nobody else's.

This wasn't the first time lies were told by my wife's family, and will probably not be the last either.

In any case, why did Wanda think that the best way to help her sister, me, and our children was to try to pull strings, which could not actually be pulled at all? She only had to ask us what she could do to help. I think it may have been because she needed to be seen to be exercising the same degree of control she did over the rest of her life, and which this time was beyond her abilities.

Unfortunately, this was the approach which was taken to me and my family consistently. My wife's family knew best apparently, even though they hardly spoke to any of us. They were always doing things to help us, they said, but we knew nothing whatsoever about what it was they were doing, when they were doing it, and why exactly. I was treated with total disdain and ignored completely.

I don't think I will ever come to terms with the way our daughter's overdoses were handled by my wife's family. I actually think that to use the word family in this context is a big stretch. I have never had so much as a tentative enquiry as to how she is doing, yet they have all known she has been in hospital, and therapy.

One member of Sam's family did once claim that they had asked Abigail herself how she was. I replied by asking them if they thought it was appropriate to ask a fourteen year old child, who had attempted to end her life, how she was, without any reference whatsoever to her father.

There were a whole string of mistruths which were used to disguise Sam's family's total disregard for us all. I am sure these continue to this day, as without them they cannot hope to justify their complete lack of care.

Chapter 11: The Merry Wanderer

'When you come to the end of your rope tie a knot in it and hang on.'
<u>Franklin D. Roosevelt</u>

One of the more disturbing habits that came along with Sam's illness was what we referred to as her 'wanderings'. She would go missing for hours at all times of the day and night, and then return in a terrible state.

I know that some of the time she would go to Tesco, buy wine, and then decant it into smaller juice bottles in the customer toilets there. She would use Oasis bottles, as the colour of this soft drink was similar to Rose wine, so she could carry the bottles in her bag without raising suspicion. This also meant she could sit on the bus and drink for long periods of time and then save some more for when she got home, to hide around the house.

Most alcoholics have a 'substance of choice' and I cannot be sure when Sam's became Rose wine. This may well relate to the ease with which it can be passed off as a harmless juice, or something else, I don't know.

The point here is that addicts rely on the fact that their drinking is a big secret. They have a very personal relationship with their substance, which they honestly seem to believe nobody knows about. I would often try to make Sam realise that it was not a big secret at all. Anyone who knew her well enough, her parents and sisters excluded, would know within a split second that she had been drinking.

I could tell before I entered the house after work, through the door, simply by the shape of her body and how she was holding herself. Other times it was just the look in her eyes or a facial expression. It never was the concealed habit she thought it was, and needed it to be.

When I explained all this to her I would tell her that it was much like living with a wife who was having a very long term affair. The difference was that the affair was with a bottle, not another man, and this made it all the more difficult to deal with.

How could I, as her husband, continue to treat her as my wife when, just as in the famous Princess Diana quote, *'there were three of us in this marriage, so it was a bit crowded'*.

I would shout at her angrily that I could live with her having a dalliance with a person far better. For her to neglect her own husband and family in favour of a pink liquid, though, was too much to bear. How could she choose a bottle over her husband and family?

Sam is probably one of the worst types of alcoholic to have to live with as, being intelligent, she could always stay one step ahead of us. This included the constantly changing hiding places for her wine and money. We would often search the house inside and out without success, only to find her drinking later the same day. I have found bottles in all sorts of places including; on top of wardrobes, in the garage, behind bushes in the garden, under my own or a neighbour's car, in the hedge at the end of the street, and even in my own underwear drawer.

You cannot stop an alcoholic drinking, they will always find a way. I must have thrown away gallons of wine but it was all replaced and drunk again, so it was totally pointless. It became a way of life for me and the children, confiscating bottles, trying to avoid any conflict, and making ourselves scarce when things got too dangerous.

We would sometimes run away to my Mum's and just leave Sam to her drinking, returning later when she had drifted into an alcohol induced coma. When we returned to the house later in the evening I would whisper to Abigail and Daniel, *'don't wake the bear'* and we would sneak into the house as quietly as possible so that we could retain some level of normality for ourselves.

Although we would be helping to save our own lives by leaving Sam alone in the house, at times she would place herself in danger. She would leave the oven or iron on, lock doors and lose the keys, or throw things around the house.

I remember one time when we returned home to find a raw beef joint on the doorstep, a cactus plant on the drive and various items of clothing hanging out of open windows. It was like a murder scene from CSI Stoke.

On returning home, despite sleeping in a separate bedroom, I would still often be woken in the night. Sam would emit what sounded like the noise of someone in childbirth, as her brain reacted to the very weird 'non-sleep' which too much alcohol would produce. This would sometimes wake the whole house and was very distressing.

When she was totally out of control Sam would sometimes sleep in her car rather than in the house. She would say I was throwing her out and then refuse to come back in. We had an allotment for a while and she would go missing for whole nights, sleeping in the shed on the plot. When I cleared the land for handing back to the Council I found countless empty bottles in the greenhouse, compost heap, and even amongst the cabbages.

She had been using the site as a secret drinking den. Nobody could bother her there at all, and I don't think she was the only allotment owner to do this, from what I have heard since.

One night she was accosted by another drunk on her way back from the allotment, but even this didn't seem to curtail her totally mad behaviour. There was never anything to be gained from trying to bring her back from her travels, I gave up on that. She would only ever create another drama on our doorstep if she was forced to come home, so it was usually best to let her wander.

Around this time Sam took the first of what was to be many overdoses herself. Maybe I had become hardened to it all, to some extent, with what I had been through with Abigail, but the shock was somehow diminished a little. This didn't mean that her life was not placed in real danger by her actions though, and there were a few subsequent close calls.

Sam's overdoses would be drink fuelled and usually take place when I wasn't around. There was a particular one which could very easily have resulted in her death, as it was her friend who actually called an ambulance after speaking to her by phone. She had taken a huge number of tablets, washed down with plenty of wine.

NONE of Sam's suicide attempt hospitalisations, or their aftermath, were ever to be attended by her parents, I think it's FOUR to date.

These incidents invariably took place after phone-calls to her Mum or Dad. On these calls she would be met with instant anger from her Mum, and twisted, sarcastic mockery from her Dad. There was never any attempt to calm the situation, or arrange to meet. I know this because I heard some of the calls, it was hard not to, as her Mum's voice in particular could shatter glass. The effect of this very angry reaction, from the woman who had given birth to her, was to send Sam into further depression and further drinking.

You would perhaps think that someone in this very desperate situation, with suicidal thoughts and actions, would be able to call on her own parents for help. However, this was not the case, as I witnessed Sam being refused any kind of assistance outright by her parents, on two separate occasions. These both occurred when Sam had returned from her wanderings and I had told her she couldn't come back in the house, and so should ring her Mum instead.

I stood with her in the drive and listened for the response from her Mum. I didn't need to listen very hard, as when Sam asked if she could stay with them there was the loudest *'NO!'* I have ever heard down a phone line. There was a similar reaction when she tried a different tack, and asked if she could just come to their house to speak to them. She made it clear she didn't want to stay on this occasion but permission was still refused outright.

This whole scenario happened again some weeks later after another return from a wandering. I still can't get my head around this, and I don't think there is any explanation which would make sense of it to me. For any parent to refuse to help in any way at all, when their child was crying down the phone and pleading with them, is beyond my comprehension. I believe very strongly that if you have brought a child into the world then they should never cease to be your responsibility.

A child is for life, not just for Christmas!

None of Sam's family have ever had the pleasure of seeing her in one of her very abusive, violent phases. I think her parents had only one situation to deal with, ever, when she embarrassed them in front of their neighbours by shouting in their drive, that's about it. When compared to the daily nightmares me and the children had to deal with this is a joke, they have completely avoided all the addict action, at the expense of just about anybody else but them. In truth, the residents of our own street have suffered much more of Sam than her own parents have.

It was much the same for Sam's sisters in that I can only recall one time when they had just a small taste of the monster she would become. I think this was probably enough for them, they didn't want this sort of thing in their lives.

In a similar way they have not seen Sam completely sober for years either. There have been no concerted efforts made to speak to her, knowing she would be in the right frame of mind to talk. It seemed to serve their purposes far better to react to phone-calls and emails, or turn up totally unannounced at the wrong time. They never asked me how they could best help the situation at all, ever.

During one of the drunken brawls we had at home with Sam, I completely lost it, along with Daniel. I angrily told her we were going to take her back to her mother, and she could deal with her instead of us. Why should her parents continue to escape all this and sit in complete comfort, just around the corner?

We both attempted to drag and manhandle Sam to my car but it was impossible. She let out one of her blood curdling screams and fought with us like something possessed. We had to give up as one of us would have got hurt.

This happened on a number of other occasions. I was desperate for my wife's parents to experience the life we were having, as they had managed to avoid it all completely, with the help of their other daughters. They had suffered none of what we had, and it just wasn't fair that they were getting off totally unscathed.

I met someone once who had actually managed to achieve what I was attempting to do. He packed up the car with all his alcoholic partner's stuff, drove to her parents' house and unloaded it all, along with her, onto their drive. Fabulous!

Hearing this made me so envious of him for being able to carry this through. Unfortunately, after attempting it myself another couple of times I just couldn't achieve it, which was a real shame. I knew what the result of this would have been anyway. Wanda would have been called in, along with the rest of the cavalry, and the drama would return to my own doorstep, with Sam as the kind of shitty boomerang.

Another thought I had was for my own parents to go to see Sam's and have it all out with them. It was totally unfair that they had to deal with some of the drama we did, whilst her own parents carried on with their lives regardless. I resisted encouraging this though, as I think there may well have been more than a little 'unpleasantness', shall we say, if my Dad had ever got to confront Sam's father face to face about how he had conducted himself.

My Mum was the nearest thing Sam had to a mother now, but she didn't get involved with any of the violent dramas. I wouldn't want her to, she was not her daughter or sister. We didn't ever call my parents in to help, and dealt with all the major incidents ourselves, or with the help of the police. This was the opposite of how my wife's parents had always behaved. They would, without question, call on Wanda's services the instant there was any prospect of a difficult family situation, and had done so for as long as I had known them.

I felt completely powerless to control Sam's behaviour. If I tried to prevent any of her crazy antics we would all have to suffer alternative histrionics instead. She was totally out of control at times.

There were a few occasions when she would inexplicably remove all her clothes and run out into the street, in her birthday suit, with all the various wobbly bits exposed to the neighbours. Frantically giving chase, close behind, would be myself and Abigail, usually at least partly clothed, but adding another ingredient to the cultural milieu of the occasion, I imagine.

I couldn't help thinking of this afterwards with the Benny Hill Show theme music playing in the background.

It seemed reminiscent of those speeded up chases with scantily clad women, which became his trademark. It would not be a surprise to me if a video of one of these naked races should appear on You Tube one day.

I tried to remove Sam's income stream to cut off her supply but she always found a way to get hold of money. I cut up her bank cards, took her purse, and hid my own wallet and keys. I could not stop her receiving her benefit money into her own account and when this ran out, which it always did, she would steal from the children. No matter how often I told them to hide their money, or give it to me, some would still go missing.

She once bought an exact replacement for Abigail's sealed tin money box, so that she could spend the contents and replace the coins with just coppers.

Sam would also regularly pawn her jewellery, including her engagement and eternity rings. I have bought them back for her many times now, increasing my own debts still further.

This behaviour was once explained to me by a therapist:

'An addict thinks only of their substance and absolutely nothing else matters, not even their very nearest and dearest. Their number one priority is their substance of choice, and they will treat it almost like a person'.

In alcohol therapy addicts are sometimes asked to write a bereavement letter to their substance, so that they can try to move on without it.

It is difficult to describe, so that anyone will truly understand, the mental torture of living with an abusive, violent alcoholic. Only those who have had to experience this themselves will ever truly comprehend, in the same way that only addicts will ever be able to empathise with other addicts.

When Sam was missing she would often send me streams of disturbing texts saying she was going to end her life, and it was all my fault. I was usually to blame, sometimes Abigail, and sometimes her parents and sisters, when it came to these threats. She would tell me which hymns she wanted at her funeral, then say goodbye and turn her phone off, for increased dramatic effect.

If she did continue to text after making her threat I would ask her what music she wanted at her funeral, and then counter her dare by saying I would have all her most reviled tunes played instead. A favourite retaliatory response from me was that I would have 'Zoom' by Fat Larry's Band played, which was a song she had always hated ferociously. She would turn the radio off the instant she heard it, so I knew the thought of this being heard as her coffin stood in church would really wind her up.

This odd tactic actually seemed to work a couple of times. She would wake up to the utter madness of where she had placed herself, and return home.

I would sit in front of the television when she was missing and attempt to remove any thoughts of Sam from my mind, but to no avail. The effect on my body during these periods could sometimes be quite severe. I would get what some people describe as a 'washing machine' effect. My stomach, chest and head would all churn at the same time as waves of nausea rushed through me. I would also sometimes develop a shake, mostly in my arms and legs, but this would usually ease once she was home and settled.

At other times I would try to carry on with simple household tasks but end up snapping at the children and then having to apologise straight away. I think they did mostly understand the pressure I was under. Even so they sometimes found it difficult to make allowances. Happily they all had a good network of close friends to turn to. Abigail in particular had managed to segment her own friends into those who knew the full story of her Mum and those who didn't, so could call on the most appropriate ones for a particular situation.

Sometimes during the long periods when Sam was missing without any contact I would plan for her death. I would think about how things would be without her around. No money worries, the house paid for, no abuse or violence, holidays, and maybe the chance to start my life again with a new partner.

This took another, darker, step occasionally when my thoughts would turn to murder. I would stare at the patio through the window and think through me burying her body under it, Brookside style. I would run through in my head having to explain to the police how she was missing again, and that I had no idea where she may be.

Apparently I am not alone in harbouring these thoughts. When talking to other supporters of addicts, in groups, many of them said they had the same feelings when at their wit's end. It sounds terrible but is just a measure of the unbearable psychological burden of living in the surreal parallel universe of addiction. It's much like a nightmare, except they usually come to an end. This doesn't.

I say addiction when referring to myself as well. To some extent, I think when caring for an alcoholic you can almost become addicted to the continual misery. It becomes a very peculiar existence when dealing with things on your own, as indeed I was for most of the time.

Chapter 12: My Canal Walk

'Never, never, never give up.'
<u>Winston Churchill</u>

Things reached crisis point for me in March 2015. I had been having a very difficult time with my new employer, a high street bank, as well as a particularly bad period with Sam, which was pushing me to the very end of my tether.

I could hear the rumble of my whole world collapsing around me, and couldn't face the thought of another minute of the desperate life I had. It felt as though I was falling deeper and deeper into a huge black hole, with no possible escape. The massive weight of my responsibilities was pressing down hard on my shoulders, and I found I could barely find the strength to keep moving. Every task seemed more difficult than the last for me, and I was having immense problems finding the energy to simply exist.

One day I calmly left the house with every intention of ending my own life. I couldn't go on with the torment any longer.

I drove to the canal, parked up, and turned my phone off. Curiously I felt empowered by my determination to do something which was only for me, and no-one else. This was now wholly, exclusively and totally about me alone, for once. I had been dragged through years and years of having to think of everybody else, including my burdensome wife, now it was my turn.

Calmly I walked along the canal towpath staring deep into this caliginous, brown trench. I began to think through how I could ensure my body stayed under the murky water, rather than float to the top, in abject failure. I didn't like the thought of drowning but knew, as I wasn't a great swimmer, this may be an effective end for me.

How could I ensure I didn't make it to the bank, and remain hidden in the icy calm depths?

Trollies! There were always supermarket trollies in canals right? I figured I could get my leg trapped in one of these if I found a good spot, and this would ensure I wouldn't be able to swim to the surface. All I had to do was find the right place, with the most urban debris visible, and then jump in, easy.

I surprised myself at just how simple I was finding it to consider the practicalities of ending my life. Part of this may have been that I had never been religious, so I didn't have God standing in my way. Many people in this situation may have taken the time to pray, but I didn't feel the need to speak to someone who had never been part of my life.

I had spent all of high school in a Catholic domain yet never really bought into the religion for myself. Once I had children I again found that I was heavily involved with 'Catholicity by necessity', as they were the providers of the best schools. There simply wasn't an alternative choice in Stoke if you wanted your children to have the best chance in life, as far as I could see. Results from other schools were very poor generally, and were ranked towards the bottom of just about every league table in the country.

I don't think this was necessarily about the standards or teaching, I have met some very good teachers in the area. I actually think it was more about the 'poverty of aspiration' which has been prevalent in the city for many years.

Potteries folk are mostly warm, friendly, salt of the earth types, but also have an inherent negativity, and quite an insular view of life. This has been augmented by the decline of all the local industries, including its world renowned ceramic industry.

Living in Stoke, I feel can lend itself very well to suicidal thoughts, it can sometimes seem like a way of life for some residents.

I don't think this helps the local educators, who must often feel like they are fighting a losing battle to implant ambition into the city's children. Of course I am generalising here, there are some good examples of how things are improving for my home city, and long may this continue.

Some may say that playing the system to get my children into a faith school is slightly dishonest. To me it was a complete no-brainer, I wanted my children to go to the best performing school in the city. Any other choice simply wouldn't have cut the mustard. This is not intended to disrespect anyone who makes a different decision. We all want the best for our children and endeavour, as parents, to be the wind beneath their wings. In my case though, I didn't want to settle for anything less than a hurricane to help lift my children to the heights I knew they could achieve. Anything less just wouldn't be acceptable.

I had continued to be exposed to religion in my role as a parent governor and had always demonstrated the utmost respect for what this stood for. It just wasn't me.

There was no animosity on my part, and there are many aspects of Christianity in all its forms, which I very much admire. However, I have from time to time found it difficult to accept the level of hypocrisy demonstrated by some people purporting to be Christians.

At school I remember I would watch the kids who went up for Holy Communion and think, surely that guy cannot possibly be worthy of 'receiving the body of Christ'. He's a complete and utter swine, and always in trouble. How can he act like a saint in church, and then revert back to his usual behaviour as soon as he leaves?

Conversely, I would witness this same, very morose girl, with the very Irish name, go to confession at every opportunity, looking like the whole world was against her. What must she have done that was so bad, for her to have to beat herself up every week like this?

Sam had faith, and had converted to Catholicism when the children were in Primary school. Religion never seemed to help her at all though. Whenever she went to church, which wasn't as often now, she would tend to drink on her way back. It was almost as though watching a member of the Clergy knock back the wine in Mass made it too difficult for her to resist resorting to it herself.

Or maybe it was a case of her exposing what she had done to herself and her family while in Church, but being unable to deal with it in any other way than to return to drinking.

When it came to my mother-in-law's approach to religion, she exuded a somewhat pious demeanour, which belied the way she actually lived out her life. For instance, she would try to make me feel that I was somehow letting everyone down by not going up to be blessed in Church. I couldn't take Communion, being a non-Catholic, but she seemed to want to force the issue of me participating as much as possible.

We went through a spell of attending Church regularly, when the children were younger, and she would stand in the Communion queue and keep beckoning me over from my seat in the pews. I rarely capitulated and would mostly stay seated, respectfully following proceedings. My wife and children would often take Communion, or have a blessing, but it was always their own choice.

As I got to know them better, it was this kind of extreme form of insincerity which I found hardest to live with from my wife's family, many of whom were practising Catholics.

Practising?! I think they probably needed to go back and start learning what Christianity was all about again, with the children in the Liturgy. They definitely weren't practising hard enough as far as I could see. The way my wife and children had been treated by them certainly didn't reconcile with anything I had ever learned myself from religion. I wonder how much time they have spent in confession in the last few years.

I never discouraged my own children from embracing Catholicism at all. In fact I positively encouraged them to take part, but I never found much enthusiasm myself. It wasn't that I didn't try to understand, I simply didn't buy into the whole elaborate ceremonialism of it all.

However, what I did understand and appreciate was the underlying teachings from the Bible, which I like to believe I have passed on my own interpretation of to my children. These are actually just a simple set of rules dictating how we should all behave towards each other. I don't feel you need a faith to be able to adopt these in your life. This is especially true of the way you bring up your children, and look after your family. It's all about being the best human being you can possibly be, or at least make a good effort to be.

What has disturbed me, my whole life, is the number of people I have met who very much acted out aspects of their religion, but have not lived out its messages. They were, to my mind, only going through the motions for show, rather than learning to be better people.

For me there was a complete disconnect between religion and the real world. I was in awe of those who had faith though. I have had friends, colleagues and acquaintances who have faith, from Sikh's to Jehovah's Witnesses, and we have got on very well. Unfortunately, I was never able to come close to seeing the light myself.

In AA and Al-anon they do say you need to find your own Higher Power, whoever or whatever that may be. Their thinking is that we all need someone or something to call on in our time of need, and who steers us through life's many problems. Without a Higher Power to call on, they say we are likely to flounder, as we are too weak on our own, and there are too many things which are out of our control, and which we need to be able to accept.

Well I had no Higher Power, so that was that!

So do I jump, or not?

Then I started to think more of what kind of mess I would leave behind. Would the children cope without me, and how would their lives pan out without me around?

Could I trust Sam with all the money she would have? What would my parents think of me? Was this a cowardly act? I was much stronger than this wasn't I? I rarely give up on anything, why am I giving up on life? I had never been a quitter, so why start now. What would this teach my children about how to live their lives?

I walked back to the car, left the canal, and drove to a different car park. This wasn't working, so I thought I could get drunk and then perhaps I would have the courage to carry things through.

Sam had attempted suicide when under the influence, so perhaps alcohol was the key after all, I thought. What a paradoxical position I had now found myself in.

I bought some lager and a takeaway, which I thought could be my 'last supper', and then moved again to a layby out in the countryside, away from all street lighting and traffic. Sitting in complete silence eating and drinking, I found I could only manage to consume two bottles of lager. I just couldn't get it down my throat. What a lightweight!

The years of having to avoid alcohol had meant that I now had difficulty drinking much of it myself at all. When you don't drink regularly you do find it quite hard to do what much of the population regard as totally undemanding. I drank 0% strength lager at home, and only because I found soft drinks too sweet, but even this only amounted to a couple of small bottles at the weekend. Drinking spirits had never appealed to me, and I certainly couldn't gulp alcohol down with abandon, in the way some people could.

After sitting in the layby for a few hours I came to the realisation that I was not going to be able to end my life.

Surely, I was stronger than this, and had too much responsibility resting on me to simply run away, as my wife's family had. They were not going to beat me, and neither was addiction!

I drove back home, to be met with an angry rant from Abigail, asking where the hell I had been all day.

Resigning myself to carry on, I came to the conclusion that I was needed far too much by my children to surrender to the immense pressure I was under. I had often repeated the phrase, *'what doesn't kill you makes you stronger'*, to myself, and found that again this gave me the energy to pick myself up and carry on.

Another one of the main things that stopped me from seeing through my demise was that I was worried nobody would really understand exactly why I did it. The life of an alcoholic's carer is a very, very lonely one and extremely difficult to explain to people who have not been in the same position themselves. There just isn't an easy way to relate it all, particularly to people who drink heavily or regularly themselves, as they will rarely get it.

I was also worried about my Mum and Dad and what they would think of me. My Mum had helped me to get through some of my darkest days, just by being at the end of the phone sometimes. My parents were getting on in years and would soon need me around more, so I couldn't just desert them, it wouldn't have been fair.

To stay alive was the only option, if only to ensure that my children understood completely why I had acted the way I had. I knew it would be a very difficult thing to explain to anyone, and who would be able to do this if not me?

I couldn't live with the thought that I would be regarded as some sad, misguided loser, who simply couldn't cope with a wife he should have divorced a long time ago.

There was no choice but to continue to fight the fight.

Giving up had never been in my nature anyway.

Chapter 13: Saved by a New Job

'After a year in therapy, my psychiatrist said to me, 'maybe life isn't for everyone.'
<u>Larry Brown</u>

Sometime in the weeks after my canal walk I received a call from a lady from a recruitment firm, who I had last spoken to me at least a year previously. She said she had finally been able to find me the job I was looking for, which met all the conditions I gave her all that time ago. I was surprised, as the type of position I was looking for was widely regarded as being 'as rare as rocking horse poo', in the eyes of both colleagues and other employment agencies.

The financial services industry as a whole was still struggling to find its way after the turmoil of the massive regulatory changes during the last five years or so. This meant that recruiters were often trying to shoehorn the available candidates into jobs which were often too good to be true.

There would be incredible promises made by some prospective employers, as they were desperate to capture the limited supply of qualified people in the market.

Understandably then, I met this offer of a golden ticket with some scepticism. Anyone who has ever dealt with recruitment firms will know that they can often be somewhat economical with the truth.

I had hoped that I could get a new job with the aim of reducing my stress levels, so that I had a better chance of coping with everything that was happening at home. I knew this would probably have to mean a reduction in my overall pay if I was going to leave banking, but was prepared for this, and resigned to the fact it would have to happen for me to be able to stay alive.

My job as a financial adviser was the type of profession where people tended to move around quite a bit. The nature of the beast was that you could often end up in an extremely stressful situation, and have to move on for greener grass. You were only ever regarded as being as good as your last deal, so loyalty to employers didn't really play a part at all, unfortunately.

I have worked in this kind of environment for around 25 of my 33 years in work. My first full time job, before I went into food retail, was actually as an insurance agent, selling promises on council estates.

I still sell similar promises now, but generally to people with a lot more money. There is no-one I can think of who has taken my advice and suffered financial hardship from it, so these pledges have largely met my clients' expectations over the years.

As an insurance agent, selling and collecting on policies meant I got to meet all forms of life, some barely human, at the tender age of 18. It was a baptism of fire, and there was a massive emphasis on targets, as the largest proportion of my pay would be commission based back then. Unsurprisingly, I never saw door to door sales as a worthwhile career so left this industry completely for a role in retail management.

Although I wasn't on the street anymore in retail, there were still big pressures. This was both a physically and mentally demanding job, with combative senior management who took no prisoners. This, combined with the awful working hours, eventually forced me to reconsider my career. I enjoyed some parts of my job but was working as many as 80 hours a week, with a significant number of these unsocial. It didn't lend itself well to my burgeoning relationship.

After spending around 8 years in retail management I left to return to an insurance sales job, and then on to work for banks and building societies. My longest stint was 14 years with one bank, where I was promoted a number of times. On average I spent around 4 or 5 years in each of my jobs, which is a pretty good average for my profession.

I have never been sacked in my life, and always left a job totally of my own volition, although Wanda likes to tell people that I have had more jobs than anybody she knows, and that Terry once *'saved'* me from being fired when we both worked for the same building society. Talk about kicking a man when he's down!

I am truly grateful if my brother-in-law did 'save' me, but can't recall when this may have been. If it were true then it would most likely have been when I was looking to move on anyway. Advisers moved around all the time, and there was obviously a tendency to switch off, to some extent, when you had another position lined up elsewhere.

Anecdotally, there have always been suspicions around the exact circumstances by which Terry came to have his 'career change' not long after I first met him. I also have good reason to believe that Sam's Mum's 'retirement' from her job may have had a little bit more to it than she has had everyone believe all these years.

Anyway, expecting the worst from the referral from the recruitment firm I went for the interview with my prospective new employers.

It was actually a revelation. As soon as I walked in I got a feeling about the place, and something told me this was it. The interview went well and was very relaxed. They seemed to like me and within a couple of weeks I had a start date. I am now in my third year with them, at the time of writing, and regard the firm as my saviour. If I hadn't found them in the way I did I think things could have panned out much differently.

I had been seeing a counsellor at the time, arranged by my previous employer. Although this was helping, I knew I had to somehow escape my current role for a more relaxed working environment, to rescue my sanity. I had made the mistake of returning to work for a bank some months earlier, simply because this was the type of job I had spent the largest proportion of my working life in, and they were offering a good salary. It had proved to be a big error of judgement. The banks were still reeling from the effects of the banking crisis, along with the huge changes they had to make under the new regulations.

This meant that being at the sharp end of all this, in a client facing position, was extremely stressful, being very closely monitored, and micro-managed to extremes. I couldn't hope to work in these surroundings with what I was having to cope with at home. I enjoyed my job but knew I would have to find a much less restrictive and oppressive employer.

Over the years, in my role as an independent financial adviser, I have advised plumbers, and millionaire plumbers, chief executives, priests, nice people with money, and not so nice people with money. I have become a trusted adviser to some, and even a trusted friend to others.

When I meet clients I always aim to get something from the meeting, if not the immediate use of my services then at least an insight into their own lives, and some knowledge of whatever is their specialism, or field of expertise.

My career has been my 'University of Life' and I feel I know a lot about what makes people tick, which has served me well. Having a good understanding of the wider world through my own experiences has helped me form an educated view on a wide range of subjects.

At times the huge pressure of working in this role within a bank became too much to juggle with my responsibilities to my family, particularly in the really bad times with Sam. I had been looking for a position with a smaller firm in the independent market for some time.

It has been a real eye-opener so far as I have been allowed to use my own mind, rather than constantly being dictated to by corporate nobodies. I wish I had made the move years ago, and under better circumstances. I have had to make sacrifices though. My Mercedes company car has been replaced by a second-hand Vauxhall Astra. My bank pension scheme given up in favour of a poor relation, but money alone doesn't buy happiness, or so they say.

Working alongside a firm of accountants means that what I have lost in terms of earnings has been more than made up for by my much improved working conditions and lower, although obviously not zero, stress levels. I am also now more local and can do the college run without impacting on my working day, which is a big help.

I still rely on work colleagues, and the office banter, to keep me sane. Without this I know I would struggle to hold things together at times. They seem to enjoy my strange but true stories of living with alcoholism. I think it cheers them up to know that someone has more to contend with, most of the time, than they do in their lives. Meanwhile I get to off-load onto them, which is very cathartic.

I am conscious though, that some people may see me as some kind of 'comedy martyr'. So be it, I will take this description over 'dead loser' any day of the week. It doesn't really matter what people think of me as a person as long as I can feel I am helping someone, and living my own life out in a fulfilling way.

Whoever that someone is doesn't bother me too much, as long as I can feel valued in some small way by another member of society, be this a colleague, stranger, or my own children. I don't care how meretricious this may sound, I feel we are all here for a purpose, so maybe this is mine.

Humour can also be used to make people think about their own lives. I do genuinely feel that my approach to life's trials has opened the eyes and minds of some, who would not otherwise have given these issues a second thought. Full and frank discussion of life's important issues with work mates, however these are conducted, I feel can often make people look at themselves. For me these good humoured conversations are an essential part of my life which I would not want to lose.

One of my more dour colleagues, who has a similar type of dark humour to myself, will end the week by announcing,

'Soon be Monday!'

Depressing? Or could this be just a poignant representation of my own feelings, at the thought of a weekend away from the safety and companionship of work. Sad, but unfortunately very true at times.

Chapter 14: The Chocolate Orange Incident

'Scar tissue is stronger than regular tissue. Realise the strength, move on.'
Henry Rollins

One evening Sam flew into a violent rage after myself and Abigail had removed some wine from her grasp. She attacked us both physically, scratching, kicking, pulling hair and throwing anything she could get her hands on. We had suffered this sort of thing before, but never with this level of intensity. She was totally out of control and venting her fury at us both, verbally and bodily.

In some ways the verbal abuse was more difficult to deal with than the physical. There was a tirade of sexual references and expletives, targeted mainly at me and my relationship with my own daughter and mother. I am sure you probably get the picture without me having to spell it out.

It reminded me of a scene from 'The Exorcist' and I half expected her head to start spinning around, spewing vomit, in the style of Linda Blair. I believe she was also an alcoholic, in real life, by the way

When people get into this kind of state they do seem to suddenly possess super-human strength. Sam was like a caged animal, grabbing our wrists and arms, and digging her nails in viciously. Even with the two of us working together we were no match for the hostile creature we faced. After grabbing just about everything that wasn't nailed down in the house to throw at us, including ornaments, clothes and various household utensils, Sam then found the ultimate weapon.

This was something we could never have foreseen being used against us in this way,

……..a Terry's Chocolate Orange.

It was launched with some ferocity, straight at the back of Abigail's head. It may have only been made of, rather nice, chocolate but believe me it hurt.

The utter ridiculousness of this whole bizarre situation does not escape me, nevertheless we were under serious threat and had no choice but to call the police. There was absolutely nobody else we could entertain turning to for help. We both knew that there was little chance of any useful support from Sam's family, and I didn't think it would be fair at all to expect my parents to have to deal with their daughter-in-law in these circumstances.

This should have been a job for her parents, but we also knew that there was no point whatsoever contacting them. They had proved, beyond any doubt, they were not prepared to get involved in any way with their daughter, or her family.

We had been trying to calm Sam down for hours and she was just getting angrier instead. We knew that in trying to carry on with this utter madness we were placing ourselves in danger of our lives, or hers.

The police came and took her away, but by the time they arrived she had calmed down somewhat. They took photos of our injuries, but I declined the offer of a picture of my testicles, which had taken a beating once again. I stuck with just letting the officer take ones of the scratches to my arms and face. Abigail had several bruises and scratches, and the bump to her head obviously. She wasn't visibly upset, I think more in a complete state of shock, as we both were.

We all gave our statements to a very nice policeman into the early hours. Jack gave his at his girlfriend's house, as he had seen some of what had happened but left earlier in the evening.

The police officer in attendance told me I had a wonderful family, and his advice would be to run away from my wife, and keep running, as these situations rarely turn out well. This was to be one of many times I was advised to do this but even after consulting solicitors, on three separate occasions, I could not bring myself to divorce Sam. It just wasn't that simple.

Our finances were completely entwined, and I had significant debts as a result of taking on Sam's as well as my own. This meant bankruptcy would be almost inevitable, along with me losing my career as a result. I also knew that she had absolutely nobody else she could turn to for help, based on the reaction, or rather the lack of one, from her own family to date.

My dilemma was not only a financial one, but more to do with the fact that divorce would not draw a line under my moral obligations. It would therefore not end the major problem for me, which was having to still support Sam. Conversely, it could potentially make things a whole lot worse, and me a lot poorer.

Although you would perhaps think that, having no previous criminal record at all, Sam would have just been given a serious ticking off by the police, this was not the case. Domestic violence had a very high profile at this time, after some very nasty stories concerning children had been in the public eye, so the Crown Prosecution Service seemed to want to take Sam's case very much more seriously.

They decided to charge her with two counts of assault and she was given a 12 month probation order, and a fine. This was a surprise, even to the police officers who had attended the incident.

Her duty solicitor could not help but see the funny side and made a point of referring to the chocolate orange regularly, throughout the proceedings, and in court. Unsurprisingly, I don't think he had come across a weapon of choice like this before in any of his previous cases.

It does seem quite funny now and I do often use humour to get through life, but at the time it was very frightening. Sam would always refer to this incident as being all about me and Abigail simply giving her a criminal record out of spite, but I still believe we had no choice.

Previous and future attacks resulted in knives and furniture being thrown at us. A kitchen knife once flew past Abigail's ear and landed in a cupboard door. Another time a knife thrown at me ended up buried in my jeans, just below my thigh. This only caused a flesh wound but if it had been launched at me harder, or higher, then this may have been very serious. The fact that this time it was only a 'confectionary based attack' wasn't really relevant.

One of the hardest things for us to handle was that when she was sober Sam very quickly returned to normal. She would act as though nothing at all had happened, and then seem utterly bemused with our reticence to pick up our lives and carry on without any reference to it.

I have tried to explain this on numerous occasions but I still feel she doesn't truly understand. She probably never will be able to see things from our perspective, just as I will never be able to fully appreciate the viewpoint of an addict.

What we had to try to do after one of her many episodes was to not immediately bend to her will, in terms of speaking to her as though nothing at all had occurred. We had to at least make a concerted effort to make her understand what she was putting us through.

How I wish my wife's family had seen some of this. Perhaps what we should have done, in hindsight, was call in the cavalry instead of the police, but how could we do this out of the blue when they had been so very distant for so long.

I was also sick of the manipulation and lies, so had no confidence in the out-laws' ability to do the right thing by us all. They seemed to be much more interested in protecting their own interests and not mine or my children's.

The most disappointing thing about all this for me was that the court did not see fit to recognise the underlying cause of the offence, and impose any kind of alcohol treatment as part of the sentence. They didn't even make any aspect of Sam's probation reliant on abstinence, rehab or counselling, which makes no sense to me.

I do think to some extent we still live in the dark ages in terms of how both alcohol related crime and mental health are dealt with. The police seem to not be trained quite as well as they could be in addiction and how to deal with it. They have very few resources to call on to help them in such cases. Meanwhile the CPS treat everything as black and white, seemingly without thinking outside the box.

Following her conviction Sam's unstable behaviour and wanderings continued, but we finally had contact with the BAC O'Connor centre about being assessed for entry into residential rehab. We both met with the assessor who had to be convinced that Sam actually 'wanted' to stop drinking. The other condition, having now finally secured the funding from the local authority, was that she had to have a self-detox week prior to her entry date.

This basically meant that it was down to me to ensure she did not drink at all for seven days before starting her program. This was because in rehab it would be ineffective to begin therapy with anyone who still had alcohol in their system, their brains would still be upside down and so unable to take anything on board.

Sam's acceptance for admission was confirmed and she was given a provisional date. I dared to allow myself to believe we were actually getting somewhere, and things may be looking up at last.

Chapter 15: Rehab

'If you are going through hell, keep going.'
<u>Winston Churchill</u>

A few weeks prior to Sam's admission date, we had a very rare visit by Wanda, and very surprisingly, she actually asked if there was anything she could do to help.

I couldn't quite believe it, as none of Sam's family had bothered with us at all since before she left to rent the flat the previous year. However, I took the offer at face value and asked Wanda if she could help me with the detox week. This would entail just sitting with Sam, when I couldn't because of work or other commitments, simply to talk and keep her away from alcohol. She would also need to be taken to the centre to be breath tested every day.

The time came for detox week and I heard nothing at all from Wanda. I eventually got an email from her, over half way through the week, to ask how it was going. I just said it was all ok, I was exasperated.

There was never any visit, or offer of one, so I had to take some more time off work and attempt to handle the situation on my own. It actually wasn't ok at all. Sam had managed to drink and I just about prevented her from failing each of her tests. She passed the final one prior to her admission by the skin of her teeth.

The day before her start date, after struggling all week, I had to deal with her drinking again. I was close to breaking point so when my Mum and Dad called to check on me they also phoned Sam's parents, in the hope they would do something. Yet again there was a complete no show on their part but some members of the cavalry arrived, both sisters and Sean, along with Wanda's daughter, who was heavily pregnant, for deflection purposes I suspect.

This turned out to be the one and only time that Sam's sisters got a very small taste of what we had been up against for so long. They had just a tiny flavour of the verbal abuse and none of the violence, but I was pleased they had at least seen something, after everything we had put up with. We haven't seen any of them in our house again since, unsurprisingly.

We had been informed by the centre that failing any of the tests would mean refusal of entry to the program. This was one of the most stressful times in my life to date and I was visibly shaking when I dropped Sam outside the centre with her suitcase. The tension and anticipation of being so close to a potential solution, yet so far away if she was refused entry, was making my life a misery.

She passed the test luckily, and I reiterated that this was her last chance of redemption, as I could not go on with the life she was giving me and the children. I told her, as I had done many times before, that she had to stop drinking to save her life, and her marriage.

Sam was greeted by some of the other clients and then ushered into the accommodation building to start her 18 week program. Contact with the outside world would only be allowed via a brief phone-call each evening, and short restricted visits on Saturday mornings.

The centre recommended that all those supporting an addict should attend the Family Support Group meetings held weekly in the evening. They had found that there had been a significantly greater success rate with clients who had the full support of their family, which made a lot of sense to me.

For this reason I had already told Sam's sisters about these meetings weeks before, but had had no contact from them to discuss this at all prior to her admission to rehab. I had started attending myself a couple of weeks before her admission.

It was no real surprise to me when the sisters didn't turn up for any of the meetings. I found them very useful myself. There was a room full of people with very similar issues to mine, and a shoulder to cry on if you needed to. The therapists who ran these meetings would also give an insight into addiction, and what particular topic was being covered with the clients in the centre that particular week.

I spoke to Sam every night and visited every Saturday, aside from the first week when we were advised not to. She told me in the first phone call that she would never drink again.

Apart from a short note from Sandra, Sam had no other contact from her parents or sisters until I raised the issue after around 8 weeks. She then received a rather odd short message from her Mum, much like a postcard, with the immortal line,

'Nothing much going on in Leek'.

This extraneous note caused some hilarity when discussed in the addicts' group meetings apparently. Much more seriously, it clearly illustrated the huge emotional chasm between mother and daughter. There was just no feeling there, and it was obvious her mother had merely felt she had to write, only in reaction to me raising the issue with her other daughters.

After discussing the lack of involvement from her family with Sam, at one of my visits, she suggested that the centre could write out to her sisters and parents to invite them to attend the Family Group. This was all in the forlorn hope that they would start to appreciate what was happening. I agreed it was worth a try.

I never actually thought any of them would come to the family meetings. In the group I had discussed this with my fellow sufferers and said that there was probably more chance of me being elected the next female Pope.

When Wanda turned up unannounced at a meeting, as you may imagine, it came as a complete shock to me. As the therapist, who ran the meetings, asked her what sorts of things she had done to try to help her sister she articulated a load of absolute piffle about how much 'research' she had done, and how difficult it was to deal with her. This was after telling everyone what an awfully inconvenient journey she had had to make to get there.

I could barely recall the last time Wanda had entered into a conversation with Sam, never mind her having to deal with her, in any way. The only 'research' she needed to do was speak to us, and she definitely couldn't have done a lot of reading on the subject, as she didn't seem to understand anything at all about alcoholism. I could take no more of this and left the meeting, as I was disgusted, mostly at the shear brass nerve of her sitting in a room with me and daring to give the impression she had done anything at all to help.

The therapist knew exactly what Wanda was doing, and so did everyone in the room, as it was obvious whose sister she was. Despite the confidentiality aspect, we had been meeting up for a while. Most of us knew each other quite well, having talked openly about our addicts, and families.

In hindsight I should have bitten the bullet and stuck it out in the meeting, as I think Wanda would have been shown up even more for what she was trying to do, in purporting to have helped her sister. I knew far better, and so did the therapist, as he was Sam's own counsellor in the centre.

Throughout the whole of Sam's stay in rehab I had no contact at all from her parents or sisters, apart from one phone-call from her father, a few weeks in. After trying to explain to him what was happening to his daughter in terms of her treatment he proceeded to tell me it was all a load of rubbish, and launched into an attack on what the centre and its therapists were trying to achieve.

I asked him why he had not visited us or done anything to help at all, and would this have been any different if Sam had cancer? His response was that his daughter would still have to have visited them, and not the other way around, even if she had terminal cancer. After hearing this I put the phone down and didn't hear anything from him again. In fact no member of my wife's family, aside from her uncle, called me again at all. Nobody even rang to simply ask how I was, or the children, during the whole of rehab and beyond.

This had been exactly the same following Abigail's spell in therapy and after Sam's court case. It seems that although my wife's family all lived no more than ten minutes away, they were quite prepared to completely ignore the situation, and all those affected by it.

I was, in effect a single parent, having to juggle work commitments as well as the children, on my own, whilst also financing the house, debts and rehab costs (it wasn't all funded). It appears that none of this was important enough to constitute a family crisis for any of my in-laws.

We were going under financially so my Mum stepped up to the mark and began helping by dropping off weekly food shopping. Without this I would have really struggled and it was still very, very tight, with less than nothing to spare.

Then there was a new problem to contend with. I got a call passed to me via Abigail one evening, and it was Jack on the line, sounding very distressed.

He had taken an overdose of paracetamol and was sitting in a city centre park. I rushed over to him and took him to A & E where I then re-lived the experience I went through previously with Abigail.

He had been in a difficult relationship with a girl with her own unique problems, and got himself into a very depressed state of mind as a result. The situation with his Mum, and grandparents, obviously hadn't helped matters either. Where would this all end?

I think it was the next day that I attended the family group. I was in a very delicate state of mind and felt on the very edge of reason, so thought that opening up in the meeting may help me.

My wife's sisters had decided to attend this meeting, one of only three in total they came to. Sure enough I shared the events of the day before with the group, and how worried I was about Jack. Wanda and Sandra sat in complete silence as I became tearful re-telling recent events. At the end of the meeting a couple of the other attendees came over to me to hug me and offer their comfort and understanding.

Wanda and Sandra just scarpered, emotionless, without attempting to speak to me at all. To this day neither of them, or their parents, or husbands, has asked me how Jack is, or how I am, after what we have both been going through.

The same can be said of the situation with Abigail who has taken two overdoses yet I have not, as her father, ever been asked how she has progressed with her subsequent therapy.

She had occasionally been going for tea at her grandparents after college but nothing like this was ever discussed at all. They carried on as though nothing had happened, which in some ways was the best thing to do. However, in their case it seemed to demonstrate that they were in total denial.

Some months later an explanation for the sisters' behaviour in the Family Group Meeting was offered to me via email from Wanda. Apparently, they had been concerned about *'confidentiality?!!!'*

When I reminded her that I was supposedly a member of their family, that there was a car park just outside where we could have spoken, and that they both had phones to call me on to check on Jack, there was no further explanation offered.

Jack could have been dead and there was no way they would have known this until his funeral was announced. What a very weird way to behave as someone's aunt, and Godmother in the case of Wanda. I don't know if they were harbouring some kind of perverse grudge against Jack. He had disowned his grandparents some time before and was not having anything to do with them, due largely to the way they had treated his Mum.

His grandfather had also said that he *'would never amount to anything'*, so he had good reason to stay away. What a thing to say about your own grandson! He still hasn't spoken to them since not long after his 18th birthday.

Jack has always been much more like his Mum than perhaps his brother and sister are, and I have often worried that he would be more susceptible to mental health problems. He had gone through a phase where he seemed to be struggling a little. He was arrested once as he had been accidentally caught up with a graffiti artist friend from college who was caught in the act, with Jack in tow.

They had both been to a party beforehand and smoked something other than tobacco, so were not exactly compos mentis when they were spotted by the police. I hated the thought of him taking drugs of any kind but this sort of thing was difficult to avoid at college parties unfortunately.

I knew he hadn't done any of the graffiti himself as art was something that even he would admit he has never excelled in. Anyway he has never been in any trouble with the police before or since. He didn't even get a caution on his record, for what in effect was just passing his friend the paint.

As for the cannabis, I have spoken to Jack at length about this since, and he seems to have things under control. I will always worry though, as I have learnt some terrible things about this drug and its effects. There was a boy at his school who had taken his own life due, in part, to cannabis.

I know that, despite what my father-in-law has said, Jack will very much amount to, not just something, but also somebody. He is very intelligent, as well as having a good heart. He certainly didn't deserve an attack on his character, abilities and prospects at such a crucial time in his life, from a member of his own family.

What has his grandfather 'amounted to' in his life exactly?

What Sam's time in rehab did do was allow me to spend some quality time with the children and talk properly, without the huge distraction of all the many dramas with their Mum. There were some things which needed to be said, and some things that actually didn't need saying at all.

I needed to try to reassure them that I was doing my very best for them, in the only way I thought I could. When I talked to them they would act as most teenagers would, and want me to keep it brief, but I was able to get them to listen to me some of the time. It was easiest with Abigail as the boys were not around quite as much.

I explained my reasons for continuing to support their Mum, and tried to give them an insight into her illness. They mostly seemed to accept this, although I knew it was a tough sell, in the light of what she had put us all through.

Jack was spending a lot of time living the teenage dream to the full so was difficult to pin down. I usually had to speak to him in the car, when taxiing him to and from nights out. He did seem to understand the situation though, and what I was trying to continue to do, but who really knows the inner workings of a brain his age.

Daniel is a man of few words. We would do most of our talking when I persuaded him to come for walks with me in our local country park. I had to, breathlessly, work the topic of his Mum into our conversation while trying to keep up with his determined walking pace. I am not as fit as I should be these days.

Abigail would be more forthcoming, and we would speak about her Mum, and herself, much more regularly. I suppose this was because I was, in effect, her 'acting Mum' for much of the time. I was the one she would talk to when she was having problems with her friends, her clothes, her hair, and even her periods. I was the one she went shopping with, listened to all her teenage angst and bought all her bras, knickers and other 'lady things', sometimes on my own.

I did ask all three of them outright if they thought we should divorce, and they would sometimes say yes. When they had listened to the pros and cons properly though, they seemed to understand why this was not straightforward, and the very tricky situation we were in, with no family support for their Mum.

Even basic support wasn't there, so if Sam had needed a solicitor, for instance, which she had no way of funding herself, I would have to factor this into my own thinking also.

What we never really had to discuss was their grandparents and aunts directly. I did try sometimes but they didn't want to hear it, no matter what I was attempting to say. In truth they didn't need to hear anything from me about them to know the truth.

It didn't need me to point out to them what they already knew. The in-laws had been completely absent before, during and after all the many life-threatening traumas we had suffered together. There was no amount of conversation that could ever hope to explain or justify this to them. They are not stupid so will be able to draw their own conclusions. I wasn't going to attempt to explain the out-laws' absence from our lives, as I didn't understand it myself.

I honestly don't know how my children will come to view this in future years, or how they will explain it to their own families when they have them.

Sam completed her 18 weeks in rehab in time for Christmas, and she was looking much, much better.

On her admission she was told she had only weeks to live due to her failing body, brain, and grasp of reality. Her assessor had told her she would die within weeks either from the alcohol, or stupidity, and could well end her life alive in a prison cell, or dead in the gutter. The change in her was dramatic at the end of rehab. Her face was fuller, eyes brighter, and those dimples were back.

Much of the reason for this was that the clients were fed really well in the centre, which had its own very accomplished chefs. I think this was due to the fact that feeding the brain and body was essential to give any chance of the therapy working. It would be pointless trying to re-train the thinking of people whose brains were starved of nutrients, because of their long-term drinking.

When I spoke to Sam she seemed contrite and remorseful. She didn't see the point of inviting her parents and sisters to her graduation ceremony though, as they had not been involved with her care at all. She did invite my Mum, the children, and three friends she had stayed in touch with. We sat in a room full of addicts and listened to them talk about Sam and how they had come to know her. Her therapist spoke and so did we, with me saying how pleased I was I had got my wife back.

Things went well after rehab and she volunteered to help at the centre, whilst also still attending her aftercare group a few times a week, and one-to-one meetings with her therapists.

I was invited to the BAC Christmas Party in Burton, as were all the other regular attendees at the family group. This was a strange affair, sitting in the middle of a very large room full of addicts, drinking only warm cans of pop. The special Guest was Russell Brand who is a patron of the centre, and recovering addict. He has sponsored people through rehab with his own money.

It was interesting to meet a man who obviously hides behind a very controversial, abrasive public image, for the sake of his career, yet actually has a heart of gold. I had never been a huge fan but he did surprise me. He did a very short speech and then spent all night talking to anyone and everyone, circulating around the room to simply chat or hear their stories.

Christmas came and went without a hitch and I started to feel confident of a new sober future. We obviously didn't have the usual visit from my mother and father-in-law, but did have a really relaxing time with the children, and everything seemed good with the world.

We even invited some of Sam's friends from rehab for a meal at our house over the Christmas period. I cooked a chilli and listened to them recount events from the centre. They had all had very serious problems in their lives but seemed to now be in control of their demons. We had a pleasant evening sat around a roaring real fire.

Sam continued attending her regular aftercare meetings at the centre, and also helped out with taking the clients for their daily walks. There was even talk of this eventually leading to a paid job there.

Things were going swimmingly and I did allow myself to dare to start thinking of the future again.

There was a lot of too-ing and fro-ing for me so I was spending huge amounts of time in the car. There weren't too many days when she would not be attending the centre. I didn't mind, though, as I would rather be doing this than suffer the alternative.

However, it was not destined to last, and after around three months of hope and sobriety, Sam relapsed.

It was devastating, and I couldn't believe that, after how well things had gone, she could return to her old ways.

Chapter 16: Back on the Roller Coaster

'When your dreams turn to dust, vacuum.'
<u>Desmond Tutu</u>

Since rehab we have all jumped back on the ride and picked up the lives we left, before rehab. All of us getting to participate in the theme park tour nobody would want to queue up for.

I have never liked Roller Coasters. I hate the thought of someone, or something, being in total control of my destiny. Having no way of steering things in the direction I wanted to go in, with no possible way of stopping the ride to get off, scared me intensely. Unfortunately this analogy represents the existence I now had with my wife very well. I had no way of knowing what would happen next in my life, except I knew it would have the occasional high, but somewhat more-so, lots of incredibly stomach-churning lows.

There was no way of planning for anything at all, from simple meals, to night's out, to holidays, as I had no idea when and how the next drama would unfold. I just knew there would definitely be one. Sam has had sustained periods of sobriety, but also spells of utter madness, which have again included her wanderings, hospital admissions for overdoses, and police callouts.

I still have a solicitor waiting in the wings to progress divorce proceedings, but I know that this would be unlikely to solve anything, so have continued to hold back on any decision for now.

Sam still has no contact with her parents and sisters, unless she phones them when drunk and in distress. I have told her family time and time again that responding to drunken calls is absolutely futile, and serves no purpose.

The much better way to deal with all this, as I have continually told them, would be to politely end these calls and then arrange a calm meeting with me to see Sam, along with her parents, at a better time. This offer has never been taken up, or even discussed, as they only ever wanted to deal with Sam as individuals, and when drunk, without speaking to me at all. I feel the reason for this is that it helps them to justify their lack of involvement with her.

It has now been over three years since I last saw Sam's Mum, which I find utterly shocking, as does anyone I talk to about this. How could any parent or grandparent neglect their own child in this way?

Apparently she tells people who ask, that I have 'barred' her from visiting our house, after one short altercation we had in my drive, when I was angry at her lack of support for Sam and me. This was years ago now, before everything went completely mad. This is absolutely ludicrous when you consider that she only ever visited us for birthdays and Christmas anyway. This was a life-threatening catastrophe we were involved in for God's sake.

I cannot think how anybody, whoever they were, could ever stop me from seeing my own children if they were in need of my help.

We had never had a crossed word in 27 years, so for my mother-in-law to blame the one time I had dared to stand up to her as the reason for her total desertion is absolutely farcical. I don't feel it is at all unreasonable to expect a mother to step up to the mark in a life and death situation, particularly when the lives concerned are those of not only her daughter, but also her grandchildren.

Perhaps even more disturbing than this was the reaction to a phone-call from my Dad to my father-in-law, where he told him I was cracking under the strain.

This was when Sam had been admitted to hospital again, after yet another overdose. I had let the ambulance take her alone this time, as I couldn't face the trauma of another torturing encounter with the aftermath of her delirium.

My Dad asked if her parents could please attend the hospital this time, and take some responsibility, whilst giving me a break. Instead, the inevitable happened, and Wanda was drafted in to go instead of them, as was the case whenever there was any parental task required of them. This was despite the fact that Sam's mother was actually visiting her half sister-in-law in the same hospital at roughly the same time! You really couldn't make this stuff up.

I didn't even get a phone-call to check we were all ok when Sam returned from hospital. Yet again my wife's family had lowered the bar.

I do think that my relationship with my in-laws could have been redeemable if only they had made an effort to speak to me, and try to understand what I was going through. Instead I can only describe their behaviour towards me, and my whole family, including my own parents, as emotionless, stone cold, and uncaring.

This was cemented by the complete lack of concern shown after all the suicide attempts, I think 8 in all, over a 3 year period. To not have had any contact simply to ask if we were all ok was beyond all comprehension. Only Sam's uncle has kept in touch and he was isolated by the rest of his family for doing so. Apparently he has been told to shut up when attempting to raise the issue.

My wife's family have done themselves no favours at all in the way they have conducted themselves, over the last few years in particular. Shameless is the only word I can think of to describe their actions.

As well as having no face-to-face contact from my mother-in-law, I have also not had any enquiry whatsoever from any of the male members of my wife's family, including those who are Godparents, for over 3 years now. Even the nephews and nieces have not asked as to my own or the children's health, although I fully appreciate that this must be difficult for them. Perhaps they are also being fed a string of lies.

It isn't only the lies which have served to inflame the whole family situation, it's also the wholly inappropriate way they have carried on with their lives in total disregard for our feelings.

I remember Abigail showing me a Facebook post by Wanda during one of our most traumatic periods. It may have been around the time of Sam's prosecution. The point is that she knew what we were going through at the time, but seemed completely oblivious to our plight in the way she acted.

The picture on Facebook beggared belief during such circumstances. It was of Wanda with her latest grandchild leaning towards a full wine glass, held in front of the baby's face. The expression on her own face seemed to be making a joke of the whole 'baby alchy' scenario. Abigail made it known how unsympathetic this was, and the post was removed without any comment from Wanda.

I have never used social media myself so I relied on Abigail to show me anything she thought I may need to know, which wasn't very often. There was another inconsiderate posting I can recall though. This one was a picture of a collection of wine bottles with a caption about how Wanda was looking forward to spending some time away with her friends in The Lakes.

Harmless enough, you may think, but very insensitive when at the time this was posted we were dealing with suicide attempts related directly to alcohol. She knew about this but expressed no concern and went about her normal business without a thought for us, as indeed did the rest of her family. I do believe that, as my wife's family are all hardened drinkers, trying to explain the relevance of all this would be time wasted.

Sam has continued to make use of all the available local alcohol and drug support. Organisations such as Adsis, Stoke Recovery, brighter futures, BAC, MIND, as well as some private therapy I have paid for also.

She has also done voluntary work for brighter futures, who knew her history, and this gave her some focus, while they had the work available for her. Unfortunately, there was not enough of this after a while, and her battle with her illness made it difficult to continue. She did get to see things from another perspective though, and learned how those much less fortunate than herself sometimes end up.

Her father had dismissively referred to her as ending up *'on a park bench'* previously, in his very disavowing way. I hoped that seeing people in this very position, as clients of brighter futures, would drive her to battle her own demons.

The most devastatingly disappointing thing about all this is that it has very often been the times when she has been receiving the most help from these organisations, when her relapses were more severe.

Basically only she can stop, and she has to want to, more than anything else in the world.

I have bought her numerous self-help books over the years and, although she would initially seem to take them on board, I would come home to find her drunk, with the books open on the first few pages. Sometimes it is the vivid realisation of the terrible situation they are in which will make an alcoholic turn to drink again, it's an interminable cycle of despair.

In a particularly low period I was thinking through any other things I hadn't tried yet with Sam. I had read things previously about people who had managed to maintain a recovery in addiction by using preventative drugs. The most common of these was known as Antabuse and had in the past been prescribed by the NHS, but was now very difficult to get hold of, and our own NHS Trust had stopped using it anymore.

The idea behind this type of drug is that once it is taken any amount of alcohol will make the patient violently ill. The hope would be that, eventually, they would associate alcohol with the violent reaction, and so cease drinking.

The difficulty was that in order to have this treatment administered legitimately you now had to have the money to arrange it privately through a specialist alcohol treatment provider. I looked into this and found that I could not manage the financial outlay on my own, so researched other ways to get the drugs.

I couldn't help but think that if this was my daughter or sister who was ill I would not be worried about a degree of expense if there was a chance it would save her life, and her family's.

My Dad had suggested to Sam's father some time before this that perhaps both sides of the whole family could put into a kitty to help Sam. There had been no take up of this idea whatsoever. My parents were cash poor, and already helping me financially where they could, so I didn't feel I could ask them for even more money.

I managed to find a supplier of Antabuse tablets on the internet and, although I had some reservations about the legitimacy of this, I ordered a month's supply for around £50. Oddly these came with a few free Viagra tablets. I didn't really get the link at first but the more I thought about it the more I understood.

To me, and I am sure I am not alone, there is no bigger turn off than a drunk woman. I tried to live by a rule that even if I only suspected Sam had been drinking I would not share a bed with her, even just to sleep, which was the normal use for a bed anyway for a man of my mature years. Approaching this in any other way, I felt, would have had the effect of sanctioning her drinking.

I am guessing that the drug companies had caught onto this and were trying to capture a market for sex starved recovering alcoholics and their partners.

Perhaps understandably, Sam would not even entertain taking any of the tablets, even when I told her it was her last resort to save her life and marriage. I still have the sealed packets of Antabuse, and the Viagra. Maybe it will come in handy one day.

I rarely drink at all now myself, in fact I find I have difficulty even watching people drink because of the very strong negative associations this has for me.

There has been an increasing trend in the UK towards people getting absolutely blottoed at home before even leaving the house for any social event. I have seen this at work events many times and now find I have no patience with it whatsoever. When tackled about it these people will say that they do it because it's cheaper, or that they need to relax before going out, or just simply, why not.

Am I missing something here? When I used to occasionally get drunk it was the act of gradually getting closer to this state, over the period of the evening socialising, which was the fun. Being drunk before the evening even starts basically means you will probably not remember anything about it at all, so why bother going out in the first place?

As for the cost issue, if you are drinking before you leave for an evening out then surely you are already spending more than you would have done anyway, no matter what the bar prices are. I can't believe those who get absolutely 'tanked up' before they leave the house don't then carry on drinking where they end up, so all this really makes no sense to me.

No sense, can mean you may be exposed to developing an uncontrolled habit, which may then become a behaviour, and then potentially, dependency and addiction.

I remember at the events at Wanda's house my father-in-law would be knocking the wine back and making ever more absurd and annoying announcements to the room. The two brothers-in-law would ridicule him the whole evening but I didn't join in. I just didn't find it funny at all. Drunks aren't amusing in the slightest. If you have had to deal with them the way I have all these years you would probably feel the same way.

I tell my children that I don't expect them to abstain from drinking as it probably won't be possible for them, and I want them to be able to have a good time, sensibly. What I also tell them, though, is that they only need to drink to the point where they are enjoying the social environment, and need to consume no more beyond this.

Drinking because you feel under pressure to do so is never going to end well. Once you start to be part of a competition to down as much alcohol as your friends, you are putting yourself at risk.

The children have all drank, but seem to be sensible so far. I can only hope they continue to be, and have experienced enough of the dark side of alcohol to retain a contemptuous regard for it.

Chapter 17: Late Night Chats with the Police

'A man's life is interesting primarily when he has failed.'
<u>Georges Clemenceau</u>

When things got too tough to deal with in terms of Sam's abuse and violence we would invariably call the police. This meant quite a few chats with various officers, some of whom would be called back for a second visit within a short time.

I did think of giving them their own house key at one point, as the visits seemed to be getting ever more regular. All this action must have kept the neighbours' curtains flapping excitedly in our street.

Each time we had these visitors, as ever, we were asked where the support for Sam from her own family was, and each time we shrugged our shoulders, or just simply told them exactly how things were. Sometimes, Sam would divulge who her sister was, being a serving police officer. We were then met with either very surprised, or very cognizant looks, depending on how long the officer concerned had known Wanda.

On a couple of occasions Sam was detained in the custody centre until later in the evening, or the next morning, but there wasn't a lot the police could do to help. They did always try though, and I have met some very good people who have all had the greatest of sympathy with my situation, and been able to understand at least something of my predicament.

We were always treated with the utmost respect and I have no complaints about any of the officers who have been called to our house. One time, when they could see that me and Abigail were both suffering a really bad time, an officer made a new suggestion to us.

Sam had attacked Abigail while I was at work. She had called the police who had taken Sam into custody. Although she was hurt, she had decided not to pursue a charge against her Mum this time. After discussing everything fully with Abigail, without my involvement, the officer had composed an excellent statement on her behalf. This made it clear that she still had strong feelings for her Mum despite what had happened. The carefully and expertly worded statement was superb and I told her so, as it conveyed the sentiment brilliantly.

After discussing the whole situation the officer's new suggestion was that we packed a suitcase for Sam and they would find somewhere for her to stay, to give us some peace. This would also give me a chance to change the locks on the house, on their recommendation. The hope was that this would maybe stir some local services into action, and she would be found a place to both stay and receive the support she needed.

This all sounded good, and although we were reticent about it, we both agreed it was worth a try.

I could legitimately change the locks as the house was now in my sole name, and I had a Separation Agreement in place. This was something I had arranged via an online solicitor, as a necessity, to ensure I didn't lose the property as a result of Sam's uncontrolled spending.
The Separation Agreement was intended to be a temporary measure to offer me and the children some degree of security. It was no substitute for full divorce, but I hoped that, as well as save our bacon financially, it would maybe make Sam realise the seriousness of her position.

She would still be entitled to her share of the equity in the house, and other assets, should we divorce. Although a half share of next to nothing is less than next to nothing, so there was not a lot to gain for Sam.

My current solicitor had told me that the most sensible settlement, should we divorce, would perhaps involve me funding a long term rental for her from the small amount of equity she would receive. These were all just thoughts, but I had felt I had to at least make an attempt to plan for the worst case scenario.

Perhaps unsurprisingly, things didn't go to plan with the Police's idea about finding somewhere for Sam to stay.

In the early hours of the next day two different police officers brought Sam back home. They had been unable to find anywhere safe they could take her, having tried several different avenues. Aside from me finding her a hotel, which I couldn't afford, we had no choice but to have her back. I never had the opportunity to call a locksmith, and it would have served no purpose anyway.

I did attempt to get the police to take Sam to her mother's house but they wouldn't, which was a shame as I felt this would have been quite a legitimate request in the circumstances. I think they just wanted to avoid a drama.

They both left, with the male officer shaking my hand and acknowledging the fact that he remembered coming to our house before, and…., *'isn't Sam…..Wanda's sister?'* .We both nodded knowingly.

We were back to square one again.

Domestic violence is very much on the radar now, and unfortunately if you are a man then you are in a similar situation to rape in some ways, in that you are almost considered guilty before you can be proven innocent. This is why I was always fearful when Abigail or Daniel were not around and Sam had one of her episodes. Without a witness I was very exposed and at risk of Sam's actions resulting in me being implicated.

During a few of her more abusive relapses I am not ashamed to say that I broke down and sobbed uncontrollably in front of her. She could literally bring me to my knees, in complete and utter desperation. The feeling of total hopelessness would well up to a crescendo inside me and I just had to let it all out. I have never been a natural crier so I can only hope none of the children ever saw me in this kind of pathetic state. I don't think they did.

What was even more difficult to accept though, was how Sam would then continue drinking, even after witnessing me crying like a child in front of her. This was the absolute power of addiction.

She would usually remember these incidents when sober, and apologise for pushing me to the very edge of my sanity. Her occasional genuine remorse didn't make this any easier for me to live with though, when I could still feel the pain. Addicts will always attack those they most care about so we were all at risk, and my family was at risk of losing me as their sole provider and carer.

Things reached new depths in September 2016 when, during a violent rage, Sam phoned the police and reported that I had attacked her.

I was arrested and taken to the custody centre while it was investigated, as per procedure. This was the very first time I had been arrested for anything in my life, and I found the whole thing quite frightening.

Staring at the inside of a cell for hours I contemplated my future, and also the terrible position my children would be in without me around. I was holding everyone's lives together, all on my own, it was too much.

When I was allowed to make my one statutory phone-call in the presence of the duty sergeant, I suddenly realised that I had absolutely nobody at all I could ring.

My parents were on their way to Derby with Jack to help with his move to University, and I was supposed to be joining them there.

This was an eye opener for me as I had never really thought through this kind of thing happening to me before. I decided the only thing I could do was to try to get hold of my Dad anyway, even though I expected him to be on the road to Derby, and so unable to answer.

Luckily he did pick up the call. I just told him not to worry, that I had been arrested, but everything would be fine.

Thankfully everything was fine, and after spending around 12 hours in a cell I was released without charge or caution, having given my statement with the duty solicitor present. The police were genuinely sympathetic as they could see what I was up against. The officers who took me home recognised the dilemma I was in, and said they honestly didn't know what they would do themselves in similar circumstances, with no family support available.

This was yet another wake-up call, and since my arrest I have tried really hard to ensure I don't expose myself to this type of situation again. If I have no witnesses around then I tend to leave the house now, if things feel unsafe.

I did make it to Derby on the day of my arrest. After my prison break I sped over to take Jack, Daniel and Abigail out for a meal and have a look at his student house, without their Mum obviously.

When I look back at some of the things that have happened it's amazing how I have found the ability to keep on, keeping on, at times.

Sam has missed out on a lot over the years due to her illness. She has not been present for some of the key events in her children's lives such as Abigail's school Prom and Daniel's 18th Birthday.

Before anything like this was arranged I would tell her straight that she would not be coming if she drank. If she did, then we would leave her behind, carry on with everything without her, and she just wouldn't be talked of. This has actually worked quite well as an alternative to cancelling or risking any further upset for those involved. It's just a shame that she has had to miss so much, particularly over the last few years.

On the other hand Sam has been around for some things, which perhaps would not have been quite the same if I had not stuck it out with her. We have still managed to enjoy some really good family Christmases with only the five of us in recent years. Sam has tried hard to keep it together at this time, even when struggling before and after the New Year.

There have also been some very simple, relaxed get-togethers at home with all the children present, just watching television together as a family, or eating, talking, and listening to music. It's at these times when I feel vindicated to some degree as they would not have happened at all if I had given up on my wife completely, as many have said I should.

I have contemplated the way my life has panned out many times, particularly when I was in that prison cell.

Where would I have been now if I hadn't married Sam?

How would my life have turned out?

I don't think there is much doubt that I would still have married someone. Having children is also something I am pretty sure I would still have done.

Would I have had more money? Probably.

Would I have had things a whole lot easier? Probably.

Would I have been the same person without my many very testing experiences? Probably not.

Would I have been happier? Who knows? I could have ended up with someone even worse than my wife, I suppose anything is possible.

What I wouldn't have had though, is our children.

With a different mother they would not be the same people they are now, and I wouldn't want to change them for the world.

Has my life been a failure so far? Not to me.

Chapter 18: One Day at a Time

'Things turn out best for the people who make the best of the way things turn out.'
John Wooden

We now all take one day at a time and I continue to live in the hope that Sam will find her epiphany. I have heard of people who have managed to stop drinking after years of trying, but they rarely achieve this without causing massive damage to themselves and their families, some of which is irreparable.

Sam recently made the mistake of telling me that she had heard of someone who had stayed clear for 10 years after initially attending 90 AA meetings in 90 days. Seizing on this, I gave her another ultimatum, asking her why she shouldn't try this herself. I said I would take her to as many of these as I could, but she would also have to get to some under her own steam, to prove her commitment.

We actually got to around 40 meetings in as many days before I decided it wasn't working. I think it was when she almost slumped onto the pavement from the car when I dropped her off for one of them. I had never understood people who would turn up for an AA meeting drunk, it was totally pointless.

I gave someone a lift home from a meeting once and he told me that AA was great, as long as you had stopped drinking. This sounds obvious but what he was saying was that you could be helped to maintain a recovery, but what AA or anyone else couldn't do was help you to stop in the first place.

No organisation on this earth could help Sam stop, only she could. What do I do? Carry on and hope for the best, or finally resign myself to failure.

There was always divorce, but I know that without her parents and sisters on board this would achieve absolutely nothing, and possibly result in further heartache, as well as financial hardship.

Sam has no-one in the world who would support her on her own and my solicitor has even warned me that sometimes the court can enforce maintenance from the ex-husband in these cases. Court rulings are often about the greater good, and they would not want her to end up on the street and be a burden to society. For this reason, and the fact that I have not yet quite given up, I will continue living the life I didn't choose, but which chose me.

You cannot Cause, Control or Cure addiction but you can make a decision as to when to stop supporting the addict, as a husband or not. While I still see just a chink of light at the end of the very dark tunnel, I will carry on. I can't say when I may reach the point my wife's family arrived at some years ago now, when they totally gave up on Sam, me, and our children.

My brother-in-law, Wanda's husband, was right in some respects when he was kind enough to remind me of my wedding vows a few years ago. Unlike some people today I do value these, and I did promise to look after my wife 'for better or worse, and 'in sickness and in health'.

Despite the damage Sam has caused me and our children I will see this out until I feel my efforts are no longer worthwhile.

I suppose at least my brother-in-law had apparently recognised that alcoholism was a 'sickness'. This was more than the other members of his family had, but perhaps it was only by accident in this instance. He has always excelled at arrogance and condescension. There is only one word which will ever come to mind when I think of this man, which I try not to. I have reserved it especially for him, and have never used it to describe anyone else I have ever known. It doesn't have many letters.

Wedding vows alone, though, should surely not be relied upon within a wider family to excuse their own behaviour. Where does simple humanity figure?

I feel both me, my wife and my children deserved far more support than we have ever had. I should not have had to offer only a blank look every time a representative of the police, children's services, school etc. asked me, who from Sam's family was helping her, and where her sisters and parents were in all this?

Admittedly, I was very angry with the out-laws at times, and may have occasionally gone too far in emails, but I was never abusive in the way they were. When I realised there was never going to be an opportunity to discuss things in person, as adults, I resorted to the only route I had left.

However, the ferocity of the response I had from them was often way over the top and, I would go so far as to say, was sometimes more damaging to me than the things Sam said to me in her drunken rages. She had an excuse for her anger towards me, what was theirs exactly?

I have been referred to by members of my wife's family as a buffoon, a coward, and unhinged, amongst other things. I have also been accused of being the protagonist of everything bad that has happened to my wife and children.

I was once threatened with violence on my own doorstep by Sean. He was very upset that I had dared to argue with my father-in-law about his lack of involvement with his daughter. This was a few years ago when Sam's father had turned up at my house drunk, while I was out, throwing pebbles at my windows to try to get someone to open the door to him.

The nearest I got to reciprocating this 'sticks and stones' approach to me by the out-laws was when I referred to Wanda as a controlling manipulator, by email. I still believe she is, and always has been, and a lot more besides, so I feel no remorse for saying this whatsoever.

The abuse from my wife's family, along with their total disrespect for me, has also occasionally included the rebuke, *'Grow Up!'*

I do find this appalling from a selection of individuals which include;

a mother who tasered her own son as a joke!! (Wanda),
a convicted drink driver, admittedly some time ago (Sean),
an unmarried mother who lectured me on marriage and morals (Wanda's eldest daughter),
and someone who had a reputation for getting absolutely paralytic at every work function, even with his bosses present (Terry).

Who is it who needs to grow up here?

Then there was Sam's mother, who accused her own daughter of harassment for merely daring to phone her, and her father, who questioned the merits of the NHS sending so many ambulances to our house, some of which had saved his own granddaughter's life.

I think it is probably fair to say that any relationship with my wife's family in the future would now be extremely difficult, if not impossible after all this. That would depend very much on them though, and certainly not me. I owe them nothing.

The fact of the matter is that there is probably no member of Sam's family who would be man enough, or woman enough, to admit they got things very wrong and offer any form of apology to me, my children, and my parents.

More recently I have been accused by Wanda of being in a 'folie a deux', which means having a delusional mental illness, jointly with my wife. I wonder who looked this very intellectual term of abuse up for her. It certainly isn't the kind of language I have ever heard her use before. Her preferred form of English could best be described as, pigeon.

There is actually some truth in the 'jointly mad' accusation, in that if you were to attend Al-anon meetings, for supporters of alcoholics, they will tell you that you are definitely quite crazy. The behaviours and mind-set you have to adopt to support an alcoholic can easily send you over the edge if you are not careful. They tell you that you need to find a way to live a life of your own, knowing that you cannot stop them drinking until they are ready themselves, if ever.

Recognising this is one thing but building a whole new life for myself away from my wife, whilst continuing to support her, and at the age of 51, is much more difficult.

Again Sam's family see this mirror illness only as a reason for further derision rather than for offering any form of support for me. Something I have had great difficulty understanding is their whole attitude towards my own health and wellbeing. They seem to regard my difficulties in coping at times as being some kind of attack on them, weirdly.

My mother once received a letter from Wanda telling her that I was having a nervous breakdown. You would perhaps think that this was out of concern for my welfare, and that Sam's family would rally round to help me. Instead, it seems to have been mentioned merely as kind of insult, as though I had caused them all a problem by daring to crack up under the strain of caring for their sister.

This attitude was also evidenced when Sam's parents once bumped into my Mum and her friend whilst out shopping. My Mum calmly stated how worried she was about the grandchildren, and my state of mind, as well as my physical health and ability to cope. There were some crocodile tears in the middle of Marks & Spencer's from my wife's mother, but nothing whatsoever came from this meeting. There was still no effort towards contact made by any of my wife's family, even after being told in a very public place just how bad things had got.

I do constantly worry about whether my actions have caused long term damage to my children, and a great deal about how they will turn out, and what they will think of me in the future. I daresay some people reading this will have their own strong views about it all.

My own parents and others who really understand the situation reassure me that my children will appreciate what I have tried to do and why. They tell me that my actions are those of a caring father and husband, but obviously I still have serious doubts about this from time to time. I have always done my very best to maintain as much normality as I can for my family. I realise that I have not always made the right decisions. Largely because it has only been me making them.

I am a single human being who has been under immense pressure for many years, so I could not have hoped to have got things right every time.

The children of alcoholics often have difficulties later in life and many unfortunately follow the path of their addicted parent. The largest proportion of these, though, also have to contend with a broken home, and only one parent for most of their formative years. I have been determined to battle these statistics and narrow the odds of this happening to my own children, by staying married, and giving them the opportunity to benefit from having both a mother and a father.

Only time will tell if this was the right decision, and it is not for other people to judge this, unless they too have been in exactly the same position as I have. Even if my thinking is wrong on this then at least I will be able to hold my head up high having tried my very best.

My hope is that by instilling my own values on my children they will turn out to be good people with a caring attitude and high morals. Unfortunately they don't seem to have a good role model in this regard from their Mum's side of the family.

With luck I will live to see them look back on all that has happened and learn valuable life lessons from it all. They seem well adjusted and the boys seem to be doing well with their university studies, so I have no cause for concern at present.

Abigail has had some fantastic exam results and is considering Criminology for her degree course. She would like to be able to get into Leeds, but will need very good grades, this being a top performing Russell Group University. She is easily capable of getting there, but wherever she ends up I am sure she will excel.

I am really proud of the way all my children have handled everything that has been thrown at them. As my Mum says,

'We Drinkwaters' are made of strong stuff.'

I am comfortable with my own conscience and do feel that I could not have done any more than I have for my wife and children. To be able to continue supporting Sam I need to live in hope and keep my sense of humour, whilst also trying to build a life for myself away from her, to keep my sanity.

I have absolutely no idea how long I will be able to maintain this as Sam's husband. My solicitor has his hand hovering over the big red button like Kim Jong-Un, but I will keep on trying until I feel I can try no more.

I fully expect to be taking care of Sam in some capacity, for the rest of my days though, divorced or not.

Sometimes I have tried too hard perhaps, and not learned from some of my mistakes. I do believe though, that this is just part of life's rich tapestry, whereas….

Guilt, shame and regrets are all for losers.

My take on 'The Three 'C's' – with apologies to Al-anon

The three C's mnemonic is an accepted way of understanding addiction, and how best to deal with it. However, I have my own view of this intentionally simplistic approach, based on my experiences.

It is undoubtedly important to help alcoholics, and their supporters, feel better about their battles with addiction. It therefore serves a useful purpose to assume an absence of cause, control or cure.

However, I don't feel it necessarily applies in every case of alcoholism. Some of these will demand a far deeper, and more complex appreciation of the individual concerned, including any prevalent underlying mental health problems.

We did not cause it

Al-anon believe that nobody can 'cause' this illness.

'Our family problems, our actions or inactions, what we have or haven't said, how we look, our past life or her past life didn't cause it. She may like us to believe they did, but not because she really believes it herself. Many problem drinkers excuse their drinking by blaming the people they love. It's as simple as that'.

However, this very sweeping justification doesn't feel quite right to me, as it offers a complete let-off for anyone who may otherwise have been held to account in some way.

It does remind me a little of how parents of small children are always told that head-lice originate from only clean hair. Everyone knows this is mistruth told to make parents feel better about where the infestations were actually coming from. It is done, quite understandably, to avoid victimising the original carriers of the bugs and concentrate minds on treating the resulting problem.

I believe that in a similar way we are completely excusing anything which may have happened in the addict's past, merely to protect those who brought them into the world, or were around in their early years.

The fact is, someone who suffers from either poor mental health, addiction, or both of these illnesses, is likely to have suffered some kind of trauma in their lives, which has made them more susceptible, unless they have a diagnosed pre-existing genetic condition.

Brains develop their cognitive ability in childhood so ultimately it is parents, and possibly siblings, who should be the ones taking the most responsibility for how someone has turned out, not those endeavouring to help them now.

Blame isn't the issue here, it's about responsibility and accountability. Acting responsibly doesn't mean an admission of blame at all. In fact the exact opposite is true. If a family wants to completely avoid any involvement with an addict in their own family, then surely they are actually showing they may have something to hide.

Family members have to forget that any of the addict's anger is directed at them, and brazen it out. For any family to try to cast blame for the addiction on someone else, in the absence of any significant evidence to back this up, is indefensible.

As J. B. Priestley illustrates very well in 'An Inspector Calls', sometimes even what we may regard as relatively trivial interactions can actually be the triggers for a major future problem in other's lives.

This can also apply to events in childhood, or beyond, which may have had a huge impact on how someone's brain develops. Choosing to deny these ever happened, or attempting to trivialise them, totally misses the point. To the individual with the illness they are life-changing events, so it doesn't matter how others may see them.

We should all therefore take absolute responsibility for what we may have said or done in the past, and try to make amends where possible. Ignoring and failing to acknowledge things ever happened is a dereliction of the duty of care of any family.

Choosing to run away from their obligations means it can never truly be said that they have played no part in their family member's path into addiction. I therefore believe that in this instance they will have not earned the right to say they have not 'caused' the illness.

As for me and Sam, if there is anything I may have done, which has adversely affected my wife's mental health the big difference is that I am still supporting her. Her parents and sisters aren't.

During a recent therapy session with MIND Sam's counsellor paused for a moment and then told her:

'Your biggest problem isn't alcoholism at all, it's your parents'

We cannot cure it

Al-anon say that alcoholism is a progressive disease that can be arrested but cannot be cured. To quote them:

'I have been presented with a problem that I can't handle so I try everything, she still drinks. I try harder, she drinks harder. I attempt anything that makes sense and much that doesn't. I refuse to give up because it makes me look weak and I know there must be something else I can do. The only thing I haven't done yet is give up completely. I know there are indirect ways in which she can be helped but being indirect they will probably not result in the instant sobriety I have been hoping to find for her'.

Although I mostly agree with this, nothing will convince me that this illness does not have a much better chance of being kept in check if there is a strong family support network in place.

Those addicts I have met who are maintaining abstinence, have managed to rebuild their lives, and in some cases their families. They will never be 'cured' in the true sense of the word, but have kept people around them who they can rely on, who act without prejudice.

I cannot help thinking that the devastating effects on my own family, including the suicide attempts, may have never have happened if there had been some practical and emotional support available, from my wife's family.

The 'cure' from Sam's perspective may have been provided by something as simple as having loving parents and sisters who were prepared to stand by her, no matter what.

We cannot control it

This one is the most difficult for me. As a husband and father I desperately want to control this illness.

Al-anon believe that from their vast experience we must:

'Release the alcoholic to find her own way to the honest desire to stop drinking'.

In practical terms I feel this is just about the hardest thing anyone can do, particularly when the alcoholic is, for a significant proportion of the time at least, the wife and mother we all love.

I have spoken to others who have managed to 'release' their loved ones. However, this has come with huge sacrifices, in that it has meant missing out on their family member's lives completely, for years, or even for good.

Rightly or wrongly, I took the conscious decision that the lesser of two evils for me and my children was to keep Sam as part of our family and live with the consequences of this.

My own interpretation of the word control was to have the ability to maintain support for the addict, whilst still retaining a semblance of normality for their immediate family.

I felt that even if we only had the benefit of some of her time as a wife and mother it would be worth it in the long run. I thought I could at least make an attempt at controlling this aspect of my life, to some extent.

Many say an alcoholic will drink on any day with a 'y' in it, and there is nothing anyone can do to stop it. Even knowing this, I can't help but think of the very basic, simple support which could have been offered to us by Sam's family, and which would have in turn given *me* some degree of 'control' over *my* life and the lives of *my children*.

Practical help could have included simple things like taking Sam to AA meetings, or coming to Al-anon with me, sitting and just talking when she was sober, giving me and the kids a break occasionally, anything at all would have helped make our lives more bearable and controllable.

Emotional support could have taken the form of just a brief phone-call or visit to make sure we were all ok. I only had my own Mum and Dad for this, as did the children.

Even if it hadn't helped Sam it would certainly have helped me and their grandchildren, nephews and niece immeasurably. This is a type of 'control' we would all have welcomed, no matter whether Sam continued drinking.

Alcohol kills families as well as individuals, but it hasn't killed mine quite yet. You will notice I say alcohol and not alcoholism, to me there is little difference, as both are big detractors in any family.

Alcoholism isn't a spectator sport though, eventually the whole family gets to play in some way.

As I have said to Sam many times, when she has been at her lowest ebb about the way her parents and sisters have behaved. They are the ones who will feel the need to lie about their involvement with us, if they are ever asked.

We, however, can just tell it exactly how it is, without a worry. I would rather not live a lie, so wouldn't swap with them for the world.

I don't blame Sam's family as being the cause of her illness, as indeed they have blamed me. However, I do feel they have inflicted further pain on my family through their complete lack of care and understanding, and their 'run to the hills', spineless mentality.

I know which family I would rather be part of and it isn't the one hiding away in their guilt and shame. They have lost out, not me.

The control I have definitely retained is over how other people view me, and how comfortable I am in my own skin. I am guessing these will be far more difficult for my wife's parents and sisters to control, both now and into their futures, in this world or their next.

Alcohol – The Way Forward?

With the knowledge I have gained by living with an alcoholic, and dealing with the various bodies involved with my wife's care, I am endeavouring to increase awareness of the issues around alcohol which can affect all of us. There are few families who have not been affected by addiction in some way, and I feel there is much more we can all do to help reduce the impact of this.

I have been lobbying my MP, Local Authority and other interested parties on the topics of alcohol licencing, education, treatment, marketing, and media representation. I feel very strongly that alcohol is attacking the very fabric of our society and needs to be controlled in a far better way.

Alcohol related crime accounts for around 60% of police time in the UK, it costs the NHS around £16 billion a year in alcohol related illness. Yet, it is still universally accepted, especially by the media, that drinking is a necessity for everyone, after a day's work. It is now fast becoming the biggest cause of cancers, including breast cancer in men and women, not just the obvious liver, throat and bowel. It will soon overtake smoking as the main overall cause of cancer deaths in the UK.

Why do we need to have alcohol available from retailers 24 hours a day? Walking into Tesco you have to try hard to avoid the stacks of beer and wine. When I was growing up this kind of availability was not around and licensing was much more restrictive. The Government have been told, and legitimate independent studies and trials have shown, that a reduction in availability results in an equal reduction in related crime, it's not rocket science is it?

If you 'need' to buy alcohol from a retailer in daylight hours you are quite likely to have a problem. Why then, do I continue to see people at the checkout buying trolley loads of spirits? I recently saw someone buy six bottles of gin, on his own, no food, just gin, with the checkout operator shaking her head in exasperation. Could retailers not restrict the sales of high volumes just as they restrict sales to those they think are under-age?

Morally, I feel the food retailers, in particular, have an obligation to deal with alcohol sales more respectfully. I believe only Asda has a policy of no floor stacks of alcohol. Why have the others not followed suit? When I worked in supermarkets, in the 80's we would have to seal off the alcohol aisles on Sundays due to the licensing restrictions. It worked fine, and everyone knew where they stood. I feel this needs to be brought back, and extended, to also curtail daytime weekday sales. If all daytime alcohol sales were put back into the control of pubs and restaurants, under much tighter restrictions, then I feel we would stand at least a chance of reducing the overall problem.

Drinking on the street would certainly reduce if this was implemented well, and I know it has been discussed in parliament and been close to being adopted in Scotland. I believe the SNP were talking of a 6pm watershed for retail alcohol sales. Perhaps it would also offer a chance for that promised land of the 'Café Culture' to flourish, with people sitting and eating with their drinking taking place in a more civilised manner, rather than falling into their food headfirst.

My thoughts are that in the same way that the US has a huge gun crime problem, yet sell guns from retailers readily, we are providing alcohol all hours of the day and night, despite knowing the much higher number of deaths it is responsible for compared to arms. We were all sold a lie some years ago when the licensing laws were relaxed. It was said we would be able to embrace a European way of life and become more like them in our approach to alcohol in the UK.

The problem is that we aren't European and probably never will be, this was a pipe-dream. We don't go out to have alcohol as an accompaniment to food, as they do in France. We go out to get blind drunk and then eat if we have to, just as an aside. It's a totally different culture in this country.

All the relaxation of licensing laws has actually done is feed the alcohol problem, particularly in the way people now drink heavily at home. It has actually had the totally reverse effect to the one we were promised, particularly as there are no 'pub measures' at home. It has to be said that this has also been seen in other countries, particularly Norway, which also has a massive problem with alcohol.

Young people are now leaving school believing that drinking is completely acceptable in every way shape or form, and have this rammed down their throats by the media and advertising. This is in some ways reminiscent of what happened with smoking many years ago, and only now is this deadly habit beginning to be controlled better.

I would ask anyone reading this to contact their MP and urge them to force through legislation to curb alcohol availability, and anything else which will help tackle this problem. There is an alcohol policy which was launched under the Cameron coalition government in 2012, but it only really scratches the surface.

Independent recommendations on availability and pricing have been around for years but not fully adopted by any government. Obviously tax revenue would be adversely affected, so I suspect this is not a high priority for anyone in power, no matter how ethical they may profess to be. They are unlikely to have the will to tackle this head on, unless pushed hard, as it is a huge earner for them, I think around £10 billion a year. It is still worth trying though, as surely the trade-off would be massive savings on the NHS budget.

You could also object to every new alcohol licence, or review of an existing one, as these are all under the direct control of the Local Authority, and not central government.

Radio 2 recently had complaints about their references to alcohol consumption. There was also some consternation about recent television dramas such as 'Doctor Foster' which have portrayed alcohol irresponsibly. It would certainly do no harm contacting all forms of media and their regulators to raise awareness and ask for explanations for their actions. I would be asking them to explain why they continue to treat alcohol as though it is a necessary way of life, and the only way to relax, rather than something which has to be handled much more carefully.

The marketing and promotion of alcohol is obscene and amounts to brainwashing. We are all fed subliminal messages constantly about the benefits of drinking in our lives, and it needs to be stopped. Smoking now has all advertising and marketing heavily restricted and yet alcohol has now overtaken smoking in terms of its cost to the NHS of the treatment for its related illnesses.

Someone who smokes any number of cigarettes on a daily basis is regarded, at worst, as an annoyance. Someone who drinks a few units of alcohol a day is regarded as a normal member of society. But someone who has fallen into dependency or alcoholism is regarded as a scourge on the planet, why?

The whole perception of alcoholism, and the stigma associated with it, has to change before we can hope to tackle it effectively. GP's are also inconsistent in their approach and will tend to differ drastically in terms of the advice they give to their patients.

Ridiculous surveys and trials purporting to show the positive effects of alcohol on our health act as a spoiler for the real facts, and are a constant frustration for me. The fact is there is NO SAFE LEVEL of alcohol, as re-iterated recently by the British Chief Medical Officer, Dame Sally Davies.

If you want to completely avoid the higher risk of cancers and many other illnesses and, of course, addiction then you have to completely abstain. This may not be workable for most of us, but why continue to believe there are any health benefits to drinking when this is just not true. The Department of Health actually does state that there is no safe limit for alcohol, and yet strangely the NHS persists with their guidelines of a few units per week. Why the disparity?

If someone was a smoker they wouldn't be told that it was still ok to smoke a few cigarettes a day, if they wanted to avoid all the possible related illnesses, so why are we still being told that alcohol is ok in smaller amounts?

I believe there should be controls on the amount of 'fake news' stories around alcohol and its effects. Whenever any headway is being made in getting the true message across it seems another story will surface about how alcohol prevents an illness of some kind. This was the same with cigarettes, and they were at one time said to improve the performance of your lungs, believe it or not. Who pays for all these fake health reports and surveys about alcohol I wonder?

This is not about spoiling anyone's fun at all. If you want to have a drink then I am all for giving people the choice, but it has to be a far better informed choice. It took around 50 years for people to wake up to the effects of smoking. We should not let alcohol take this long.

Stoke-on-Trent was recently listed in a Public Health England league table as having the second highest alcohol related mortality rates in the UK. However, it has no effective, fully targeted, integrated alcohol policy for the city, no residential rehab for 30 miles, now that the BAC O'Connor centre has had its funding removed, and very scant, underfunded and over-stretched alcohol treatment available.

Alcohol therapy, counselling and rehab does work for many people so I do feel that much more money needs to be directed towards these. It really shouldn't be left to charities and self-funding organisations to offer treatment for addiction. This is much the same with Mental Health care, which every government seems to say they are going to address but nothing much changes.

For our young people, I feel the situation is very dangerous. Alcohol is now regarded as THE 'gateway' drug, and not cannabis as is widely thought. This means that in allowing drinking to become more and more acceptable as a way of life from a young age, we are exposing this and the next generation to more risk of addiction to harder drugs.

I feel it is about time all this was taken far more seriously by both national and local government. I honestly believe we are in danger of creating a vacuous society of automatons, bereft of thoughts or feelings, and living only for their next fix.

Alcohol has been used in the past to keep the masses in check and I think it still is now. The way alcohol is embedded into our existences reminds me a little of some of the dystopian novels such as Brave New World and 1984. I actually think we are a lot closer to these scary forecasts of our future than many may want to believe.

Even if we aren't, do we really want to continue to allow alcohol to remain almost totally uncontrolled, and suffer the continuing, spiralling cost to the Police and NHS, let alone the huge impact on society and families?

Alcohol really is the gift that keeps on giving.

Why take the risk of things getting even worse for both our generation and the next?

Epilogue

'Everything is OK in the end. If it's not OK then it's not the end.'
Anonymous

As I was just about to publish this book my family had another traumatic event to contend with. This one could be classified in the, 'just when you thought nothing else could possibly happen' category, so I thought it was important that it was included.

Sam had been drinking very heavily for almost 4 weeks, which was more than she had for a long time. She had increased her intake so much that a high proportion of this period had been spent in a complete stupor, barely leaving her bed, or the sofa. She seemed to be giving in to her demons more than she had for some time, and it felt to me like the light in her eyes was going out.

The AA meetings had ceased completely, although I take some of the blame for this as I had become disillusioned. I didn't feel she was buying into the messages, and was simply going through the motions.

She had only been leaving the house for more wine, which was a significant deterioration in her behaviour, as she usually had something else going on. Most weeks there were meetings of some kind, or coffee with a friend, or a trip to the library, but none of this had happened recently.

In the small windows of time when she was both awake, and sober, she was argumentative, as ever, and wouldn't stop talking about every single ailment she had. I explained that all these other health problems would improve if she would only stop drinking. She had been prescribed drugs for her arthritic knee, along with painkillers, but these were not helping. The alcohol was cancelling out their effects.

Her constant references to minor illnesses was very much like an extreme form of hypochondria. I think what it was really about was Sam trying to give herself justification for her drinking, which she saw as the ultimate painkiller. The eternal vicious circle again.

In the fourth week of this extended binge Sam looked to be recognising how far she had fallen into darkness. I had been angry with her for much of this time and told her she was walking a tightrope and needed to do something very different, very quickly. She relented, or at least gave the impression she had, and informed me she had booked an appointment with Lifeline, a newer local alcohol support organisation, who were more strongly linked with other local health services, including our own NHS Trust.

I pleaded with her to force the issue of preventative medication this time, as I had heard that there may be a chance of this being available, if used under their jurisdiction.

The day after Sam told me she had met with Lifeline I arrived home from work, hoping to find she was following their advice. There was another meeting arranged in the next ten days or so, she said. She would, of course, need to detox to be able to use the drugs at all.

As I came through the front door I caught sight of Sam walking upstairs from the hallway. I thought nothing of it and carried on with my usual routine downstairs. Then Abigail called me up to the landing and I sensed that something wasn't quite right. When I joined her at the top of the stairs she said her Mum was acting very strangely and I should come and see her.

Sam was acting very much more than just strangely. She was opening cupboards and drawers whilst muttering to herself continually. Items from around the bedroom were being picked up, inspected closely, and then placed carefully somewhere else.

She wouldn't look at me when I asked what she was doing so I moved closer and asked again, and again. There was still no response so I stood in front of her and held her by her shoulders. Sam's eyes were staring at me, but there was nothing behind them at all. She was in some sort of trance-like state and didn't recognise me or Abigail.

This wasn't any type of drunken demeanour I had ever witnessed, and I knew there was a good chance she hadn't been drinking that day anyway, following our conversation the previous evening.

Things began to get more disturbing as Sam started to repetitively move the same things around, look under and over things and poke determinedly at the designs on the quilt cover, and her pyjamas, totally oblivious to me and Abigail. We both carried on trying to attract her attention but she would only briefly look at us in a sort of zombie fashion. It just wasn't her at all.

Abigail phoned 999 as it was becoming frightening. I explained what was happening to the operator. She didn't say so, but when I told her about the alcoholism, I knew what the lady at the end of the phone was thinking. This was a very serious case of alcohol withdrawal.

I was asked to feel Sam's back to try to judge her temperature. She was clammy and the top half of her body was shaking. We were told to watch her closely and the ambulance would be on the way.

When the two paramedics arrived a short time later we all spent some time trying to get Sam to sit down on our bed so that they could assess her properly and do all the necessary tests. She didn't want to comply at all, in fact she had no idea what we wanted her to do, as she was inhabiting a parallel universe.

Getting her into the ambulance was going to be difficult, but while we were thinking how we could best achieve this, Sam suddenly brushed past us and ran downstairs like a whirlwind. How she accomplished this, on automatic, I don't know, but after we had prised her away from the kitchen drawers we attempted to walk her out of the door.

Sam was guided into the ambulance eventually, after first watching her write hieroglyphics on a frantically sourced piece of paper. This was seriously weird, much like ghost-writing except none of what she was writing constituted discernible words of any kind.

After a struggle to strap Sam in, we set off for the hospital, with me in the back of the ambulance. She fought to escape her shackles and would not settle down on the bed, staring wildly around at the equipment and tugging hard at all the many pipes and cables. I had to help when a drip feed needed to be put in Sam's wrist. She was flailing around and it was impossible to secure an accurate insertion, so I had to hold down her arm with some force.

Only a few minutes into our journey Sam's body suddenly tightened, stretched and lifted up from the bed. Her head jerked back sharply and she let out a loud moan, much like a distressed wild animal. She shook violently from head to toe and blood started to froth and pour from her mouth, down the side of her face, and then onto the floor.

The paramedic shouted to the driver to pull over as the motion of the vehicle was making things too difficult. We eventually stopped on one side of the A50 dual carriageway so she could get to work on Sam, and the driver came into the back to help. While he operated the suction pipe to remove blood from her mouth his colleague attempted to insert a tube down Sam's nostril into her throat. It looked far too big to fit and the task seemed impossible to me.

She explained as she did this that Sam had bitten her tongue and this was to help her breathe. The first attempt at the procedure didn't work so she had to try again with the other nostril. This time it went in and an oxygen mask was placed over her face.

It was only at this point that I allowed myself to catch a breath properly as I felt the situation was now under a degree of control. Sam continued to fight with her captors, and all the equipment, including her own oxygen supply which she kept trying to remove.

The seizure had subsided after around 40 seconds, apparently, but it felt longer. We recommenced the journey to hospital, sirens blaring.

On arrival at A & E I thanked the paramedics for what they had done. I don't know how they do the job they do, day in, day out.

One of them, totally unprompted, said,

'Alcohol is the worst poison in the world'

He said he had seen some awful things it had done to people, and he had lost his own cousin to alcoholism at the age of only 33. I agreed with him, obviously, and told him that I thought a video of what had just happened in the ambulance should be shown in schools, he concurred. What I was actually also thinking at the time was that the same video should be shown to Sam's parents and sisters.

His description of alcohol concurs with my own thoughts. Some people refer to it as 'the devil's poison', which is also a fitting expose of this treacherous substance.

One of the main differences between alcohol and other poisons is that it purports to be something it isn't, whereas you know and expect what you get with the others. It cons everyone in the world into believing it is a totally harmless, life-enhancing necessity, then, when they are at their weakest, it pounces on its prey without mercy.

In the hospital I noticed a tangible improvement in the way both me and Sam were cared for, compared to when we had last gone through this with her previous seizure 9 years or so previously.

Back then there had been an air of disapproval, or possibly even contempt, from the nurses and consultants. This time it definitely felt like we were being looked after in exactly the same way as any other patient was. There were no looks of disgust or scornful whispering.

I think this improvement had probably had to happen to some extent, due to the immense numbers of people now being treated for alcohol related issues. There has been a gradual acceptance over the last decade that alcoholism IS an illness so should not be treated differently to any other. If it isn't an illness why would anyone make a conscious 'choice' to put themselves in the position Sam was now in?

Every member of staff I spoke to in hospital had suffered a bad experience with alcohol, be it a family or friend's death, or a marriage break-up. No health service in the world can afford not to deal with alcohol related conditions in much the same way it does cancer now. Why would they when it affects as many lives directly, probably more.

I spent most of the night at the hospital and had to continually restrain Sam as she wouldn't lie down. It took two of us, myself and a nurse, to keep her from getting up. After realising we weren't succeeding I asked if she could have something to calm her down.

As well as trying, with all her strength, to leave the bed, she was also speaking, incomprehensibly. I have no idea what she kept asking me for as she was not using any words I recognised. She was also clawing at the bed sheet and pulling out the monitor cables.

She would also continually pull the oxygen tubes from her nose and shuffle up and down. This meant I spent a lot of my time replacing the supply and repositioning her on the bed. I also had to get her to take some tablets when the nurse was at the point of giving up, she kept forcing it back out between her lips.

When Sam became very agitated again, and was pushing hard against me with all her might, I had to be rescued by a male nurse. The staff decided they would have to have her sedated further for her own safety. They actually got the consultant to agree to a double dose and Sam was at last calm enough to go to sleep.

I left her once she was asleep, after first warning the nursing staff she may be a danger when she woke up. Abigail was due at college that morning so I went home and grabbed a couple of hours sleep.

Next morning I returned to the hospital where a meeting had been arranged for Sam with the Alcohol Liaison Team. This was a new thing, and certainly hadn't been available 9 years ago. It was a local initiative in an attempt to make alcohol treatment more joined up.

The downside is I know the money they were using for this had come from other local alcohol services which had been closed, for example the BAC O'Connor Centre who had all their funding removed.

Anyway, we both met the two ladies concerned and had a good talk about where Sam was at with her drinking, and how things could possibly be helped. I went through what had been tried before and her long history of addiction. They did know their stuff but it wasn't long before everyone in the room realised the inevitable. Sam was the only one of us who could stop her drinking now.

We returned home soon after the meeting, I think they may have kept her on a ward for a while normally, but there were no beds available so Sam just got a prescription instead.

At home Sam was struggling somewhat with her lucidity. Sometimes she seemed fine and at other times she would be making very strange comments which had no link to reality. She also seemed to still be hallucinating and was talking to herself. Her speech was extremely slow and laboured, although some of this may have been due to the damage to her mouth and tongue.

Sam's brain had obviously not yet recovered and I suppose this was going to take some time. It had suffered serious trauma so some of her symptoms were quite similar to those of a stroke.

If this all sounds very matter of fact then it is only because the years of living through this type of drama have possibly nulled my senses. What I can say though, is that the image of my wife's face covered in blood with the tube through her nose will stay with me forever, along with some of the other visual treats she has given me over the years.

There is a reason for optimism though, believe it or not. When Sam had her seizure 9 years ago she managed to re-boot her life and keep away from alcohol for 2 years. With luck, the parts of her brain poisoned most by the alcohol will now have died, just as she almost did, and she will be able to re-learn how to control her addiction.

This is, of course, probably total rubbish with no basis in medical fact whatsoever. However, I saw what happened last time and just maybe the outcome can be similar, even if the science doesn't stack up.

I will keep going, as usual, and see what fate has in store.